LIVING TIBET

The Dalai Lama in Dharamsala

DEDICATION

In appreciation to my parents, George Frederick Warren and Ann Fusek Warren.

Bill Warren

In memory of Anthony Damiani, inspired teacher and founder of Wisdom's Goldenrod Center for Philosophic Studies in upstate New York.

Nanci Hoetzlein Rose

ACKNOWLEDGEMENTS
With special thanks to the Office of His Holiness the Dalai Lama, to Terrance John for design, and to Susan Kyser for copy editing. Additional gratitude to Saga Ambegaokar, Christine and Jeffrey Cox, Jay Cox, Michael Faber, David Grewe, Lawrence Hoetzlein, Khamtrul Rinpoche, Alexandre Kosarov, Tim McKinney, Ven. Tsering Namgyal, Palden Choedak Oshoe, David Patt, Sidney Piburn, Geshe Sonam Rinchen, Ruth Sonam, Robyn Wishna, and the warm and generous people of Dharamsala, who contributed with enthusiasm in so many ways.

LIVING TIBET

THE DALAI LAMA IN DHARAMSALA

PHOTOGRAPHS BY BILL WARREN

TEXT BY NANCI HOETZLEIN ROSE

FOREWORD BY H.H. the DALAI LAMA

Vibrant skies and morning mists surround the Dhauladur mountain range in the Indian Himalayas, home to the 6,000 Tibetan refugees settled in Dharamsala.

Snow Lion Publications
P.O. Box 6483
Ithaca, New York 14851
USA
tel.607.273.8519

Designed by Terrance John

Color separations and printing
by Shepard Poorman
Communications Corporation
Indianapolis, Indiana

Library of Congress
Cataloging-in-Publication Data
Warren, Bill, 1952-
    Living Tibet: the Dalai Lama in
    Dharamsala/photographs by Bill
    Warren; text by Nanci Hoetzlein
    Rose.--1st ed.
        p.   cm.
    ISBN 1-55939-042-5
    1. Buddhism--India--Dharamsala.
2. Tibetans--India--Dharamsala--
Religion. 3. Bstan- 'dzin-rgya-mtsho,
Dalai Lama XIV, 1935- 4. Dharamsala
(India)--Religion. 5. Buddhism--China--
Tibet. 6. Buddhism--India--Dharamsala
--Pictorial works. 7. Tibetans--India--
Dharamsala--Religion--Pictorial works.
8. Bstan- 'dzin-rgya-mtsho, Dalai Lama
XIV, 1935- --Pictorial works.
9. Dharamsala (India)--Religion--
Pictorial works. 10. Buddhism--China--
Tibet--Pictorial works. I. Rose, Nanci
Hoetzlein, 1951- . II. Title.
BQ7594.D53W36   1995
294.3'923'0954552--dc20

Wearing the mask of the hermit Dhangsong in the opera Sugkyi Nyima, a performer from the Tibetan Institute of Performing Arts coordinates movements of the bell and hand drum used by many Tibetan Buddhists for daily religious devotions.

CONTENTS

A young boy waits in line to be blessed by the Dalai Lama
during Losar (Tibetan New Year).

THE DALAI LAMA

FOREWORD

Since arriving here in 1960, in the early days of our life in exile, Dharamsala has been the head-quarters of the Tibetan Administration. Over the years, stable settlements have been created and along with them schools, medical facilities and religious and cultural institutions have been established. In the monasteries and nunneries of all our spiritual traditions, educational and training programs have been resumed and in many places improved and extended. Many monastic institutions also provide their students with acquaintance with modern subjects. In addition, many artistic skills such as painting, metal work, woodcarving and sacred dance traditions have survived and are being passed on to new generations.

Perhaps most important of all, the Tibetan sense of identity, spirit and determination to achieve freedom have not weakened. Even after more than thirty years of military occupation, people in Tibet continue to demonstrate against Chinese rule. Many of these demonstrators, like their brothers and sisters born in exile, are too young to have ever known the old Tibet. Yet they all have no hesitation in asserting their Tibetan nationality and claiming their right to freedom and justice.

This illustrated book focusing on the life of Tibetans in Dharamsala reveals many facets of our life as refugees. I congratulate photographer Bill Warren and author Nanci Hoetzlein Rose for their efforts, and trust readers may be inspired to lend their support to our efforts to gain a fair hearing for Tibet.

December 30, 1994

The Dalai Lama of Tibet, 1989 Nobel Peace Prize laureate, has dedicated his efforts in Dharamsala to compassionate living and the survival of Tibetan culture.

11

PAGES 10-11: A roaring New Year purificatory fire, prepared each March by monks from Namgyal Monastery, blazes near the entrance to the Buddhist School of Dialectics. PAGES 12-13: A young boy, gazing through colorful banners imprinted with Buddhist prayers, watches Tibetan New Year festivities. Each year for centuries, rows of prayer flags have been placed in locations where their sacred phrases can be carried on the breeze to benefit others. PAGES 14-15: Hundreds of monks gather in Dharamsala for a candlelight vigil in November of 1994 to plea for the return of a free Tibet. LEFT: Passengers aboard a local Dharamsala bus at McLeod Ganj prepare to leave for the city market.

DHARAMSALA
The Dalai Lama's Home-in-Exile

From the northern Indian trading village at Dharamsala, I hiked up a mountainous incline to the upper level of McLeod Ganj, the previously abandoned British hill station now inhabited by Tibetan refugees. The monsoon season was to begin at any time, and I was anxious to cover as much ground as possible while the skies remained clear.

ABOVE: Deep blasts from two ritual long-horns reverberate throughout the mountains from above the Central Cathedral courtyard, across from the Dalai Lama's residence. RIGHT: After placing a red protection string over his visitor's head, five-year-old Tenzin Chopak, reincarnation of the Dalai Lama's late senior tutor, Kyabje Ling Rinpoche, gives a blessing while his teacher looks on.

Once past a row of colorful stalls filled with produce, trinkets and dry goods, I stopped at a bend in the rough road and allowed myself to gaze upon the scenic Kangra Valley. After climbing further, I was able to finally meet an 83-year-old nun who lived beside a small Buddhist monastery on a cliffside, where she chanted, prayed, and rotated a ritual drum between her small, gnarled fingers.

The aging nun was one of the few women in the Tibetan refugee community who performed complete ritual pratices alongside men in the temple. She spoke no English, but through a Tibetan interpreter she said, "I came to this part of India on pilgrimage, before the trouble in Tibet. People advised me to stay here in India. I was fortunate to receive private teachings from His Holiness the Dalai Lama when he first came to Dharamsala."

A few dozen yards above the elderly woman's rickety hut, a handsome young opera star repeatedly rehearsed complicated footwork beneath a charming, stylized costume that required him to simultaneously move as both a hurried horse and its noble rider. Often, after visiting the nun who had become my friend, I would quietly find a seat in the simple theatre and observe members of the Tibetan Institute of Performing Arts prepare an upcoming concert. It was inspiring to see traditional opera maintained amidst the stark realities of refugee life.

During our six months in Dharamsala in 1990, my husband and I worked on various projects while our three children attended an otherwise all-Tibetan school as day students. The Tibetan Children's Village is one of several resident facilities for refugee orphans and other youngsters who have escaped occupied Tibet or have been born in exile.

Throughout the monsoon season, it was not uncommon to see students join together with the adults who lived with them rebuild mud and rock dams that protect the school grounds from flooding.

In the marketplaces at Dharamsala and McLeod Ganj, men with prayer beads draped about the wrist opened their outdoor shops early each morning, and women wearing long, elegant wrap-around dresses, with hearty infants strapped conveniently to their backs, spun hand-held prayer wheels while walking to the temple or to the workplace. Above the bustle, Buddhist chants could be heard throughout the day and into the evening.

This is the closely knit and picturesque community called Dharamsala, where more than 6,000 Tibetans live alongside 9,000 North Indians. To inhabitants, the word Dharamsala refers to an isolated cluster of separate villages climbing the Dhauladur mountain range to reach a height of nearly 8,000 feet. The Tibetan refugees reside principally in the old British hill station of McLeod Ganj, but the lower village of Dharamsala proper is also vibrant with Tibetan life. In a structure

that seems to rest precariously on a level site between Dharamsala and McLeod Ganj, the 14th Dalai Lama of Tibet, recipient of the 1989 Nobel Peace Prize, lives modestly as the spiritual and temporal leader of the Tibetan people.

The culture here is an intriguing mix of North Indian and Tibetan. But it is the Tibetan tradition, preserved as completely as possible in exile, that most attracts visitors to the region. From cow herder to aristocrat, the Tibetan people have been continuously relocating — mainly by foot across frigid Himalayan passes — to escape persecution by communist Chinese invaders for nearly four decades. I personally recorded several first-hand accounts of severe hunger, repression,

MAP: Dharamsala is located in northern India, approximately 300 miles north of the capital city of Delhi. The Indian government made the land available to Tibetan refugees in 1959. ABOVE: A lone cow and numerous refugees share the road in the business district of McLeod Ganj. Tibetan Buddhists in exile respect the Hindu tradition of allowing cattle to wander freely. RIGHT: Monks, whose maroon and yellow robes present a colorful contrast to a rain-soaked street of McLeod Ganj, return from an afternoon of teachings by the Dalai Lama.

21

inhuman treatment, and brutal tortures suffered by Tibetans held for up to 25 years in Chinese prisons established in Tibet during the Cultural Revolution.

It is the fortunate who can escape to a life in exile. Settling in regions just south of the Tibetan border, such as Nepal, Bhutan, Sikkim, and especially India, Tibetans have created one of the most successful refugee cultures in the history of the world. And it is at Dharamsala, located approximately 300 miles north of Delhi, India's capital city, that refugee efforts are coordinated by the Tibetan government-in-exile.

Tibetan life, with its traditional forms of art, medicine, and philosophy based on a unique national Buddhism, endures as it has for centuries. But changes, designed to foster success in the modern world, are actively pursued. Monks wear watches now, and Tibetan nuns are steadily rising in scholastic and spiritual status. The national identity is gradually changing. Computers are slowly entering select administrative offices, and a government-in-exile jeep makes Western medical care accessible to those in need.

ABOVE: Living in a 10-foot square hut in the hills above McLeod Ganj, Ven. Jampa Tenzin is one of three recluses tested by Harvard researcher Dr. Herbert Benson to determine the effects of meditation on the body. The miniature skeleton on the wall is a common symbol of life's impermanence. LEFT: Charged by an intensity tempered with a rare serenity, the late Lama Tashi, founder of the Dip Tse Chok Ling Monastery, recites his morning prayers. The lama, who lived in semi-isolation, was daily tended by his closest student of 25 years during the final months of his life. The hidden monastery, located beneath a cliff in McLeod Ganj, retains the devotion and peacefulness of its founder.

The Tibetan people have become famous worldwide for an uninhibited warmth and natural generosity. Sacred objects and spiritual practices permeate this earthy lifestyle, but religious talk is not the focus of everyday life. Hospitality is the key to happy relationships — and visitors are generally made to feel like honored guests.

My own experience found me repeatedly in the homes of Tibetans who treated me like a long-lost friend. I sat on the porch of an elderly man who animatedly told his life story and its connection to Tibetan lore. I arrived unannounced at hermits' huts and arranged to interview cloistered masters. I endured the endearing antics of child monks while teaching English language classes, and laughed with Tibetan women outside their shops and restaurants. And always, whenever practical, I was offered a cup of steaming tea, either sweet and milky in the Indian-British tradition, or buttered and salted according to Tibetan taste.

After several months in Dharamsala, I was joined by photographer Bill Warren, whose earlier travels in Ladakh inspired him to photograph Tibetans and their complex culture in Dharamsala. Together we were welcomed into one family's crowded living room, where huge bundles of brightly colored yarn were sorted, strand by strand, by members of three generations. We were invited into the rented room of a young male artisan who affixed semi-precious stones onto bronze statues of Buddha, and we watched as a middle-aged lay woman entered a mediumistic trance in her home built of discarded shipping materials.

Most memorable were my personal meetings and group encounters with His Holiness the Dalai Lama. While it is difficult to secure a private audience with this dynamic public figure, the Dalai Lama is more accessible to the people than most world leaders. He schedules open receptions outside his private residence, where he stands for many hours shaking hands with each of the hundreds who wait in line, while his quick laughter rolls forth in unselfconscious mirth. Experiencing a crowd quietly anticipating His Holiness' arrival is as moving as catching the glint in his own bright eyes, barely visible beneath tinted eyeglasses.

The Dalai Lama continues to ignite the Tibetan masses with hope in the face of nearly insurmountable political difficulties. To unify his scattered people during the diaspora, the Dalai Lama established numerous legislative branches and institutions in exile. Built into the structure of his administration in India is a means by which Tibetan culture can be better preserved in exile than within the actual homeland of Tibet itself. This alternative government provides a network of support for six million Tibetans throughout the world, including Tibet.

Dharamsala's tourists come for a wide variety of reasons. Some are trekkers tackling the challenges of nature in the Dhauladur spur of the Himalayas. An informal network of international hikers and climbers knows that McLeod Ganj, with its eclectic mix of cafes and guest houses, is a pleasant and practical place to meet fellow climbers. An apparently unlikely combination of explorers will often gather at a local cafe to chat and adjust gear prior to an expedition.

Others are attracted to the charm of Tibetan culture, staying to fully experience the performing and visual arts, infrequently seen in the Western world. Carpet weaving is a major trade; in lively handicraft centers the deft fingers of women rapidly weave intricate patterns on large looms, while men with scissors sculpt and trim the completed carpets. Infants sleep in baskets near their artisan mothers, and preschoolers play in nearby nurseries.

Many visitors come to Dharamsala in sympathy for the political plight of Tibetans, arriving to provide grass-roots

ABOVE: A large fiberglass mask of ancient design is painted by an apprentice at the Tibetan Metal Works and Handicraft Center, in lower Dharamsala. Most training in the visual arts has now been relocated to the Norbulingka Institute for Tibetan Culture. BELOW: Fresh fruits and vegetables add color to the business district of McLeod Ganj. RIGHT: While her youngest child sleeps on her back, a Tibetan mother churns butter in her family's one-room home. The butter will be added to salted tea for a traditional hot drink.

assistance in offices, homes and schools. And still larger numbers travel to Dharamsala with personal and professional interests in Tibetan Buddhism, either enrolling in classes at the Library of Tibetan Works and Archives, or turning directly to the large monastic and lay religious community. Travelers often stay several months, or even years, as volunteers or students. Both groups, often with overlapping goals, gain firsthand familiarity with the esoteric Buddhist ideal of compassionate living.

For myself, as for so many others, a visit to Dharamsala means inspiration for a lifetime. Some travelers are visibly moved to new depths, while others are transformed subtly, even without their own knowledge. It has much to do with the Dalai Lama, most will say. Something rather magical takes place in Dharamsala. Tibetan refugees continue to work diligently, proving to the world that with determination and a mind open to change, debilitating hardships can indeed be overcome. In Dharamsala, the people of Tibet have retained a natural spontaneity combined with refreshing humility, a direct reflection of the ancient Buddhist culture from which they come.

AN EARLY CIVILIZATION RELOCATES

Tibet is an oval-shaped country at the earth's highest altitudes, enclosed by the mammoth Himalaya, Kunlun and Karakorum mountains on three sides. As a result, Tibetan society remained largely isolated from the world, by both geography and choice, from its earliest history. Three quarters

of Tibet's five hundred thousand square miles lie hidden at a height of sixteen thousand feet or more. Only the valleys in the country's southern quarter are cultivated. China sits in a semicircle above Tibet's northern border. Pakistan lies to the west. India, Bhutan and Nepal border Tibet to the south. Burma rests at the southeastern edge of the frontier. The Tibetan people have always maintained their own language, government, and culture.

In 1950, the Chinese People's Liberation Army aggressively crossed the eastern border of Tibet and quickly subdued Tibetan military resistance. They imposed a peace settlement that promised the preservation of Tibetan culture and the continuation of Tibet's right to govern itself. Soon it became clear, however, that communist China meant to impose an unwelcome ideology on the Tibetan people. Armed Tibetan resistance began in the east in the mid 1950's, and the popular uprising reached a climax on March 10, 1959, in a massive demonstration in Lhasa, the country's capital.

When rumors swept the city that the Dalai Lama was about to be kidnapped and carried off to China, thousands of Tibetans congregated at his summer residence to show their solidarity and to protect him. As tensions mounted and the Chinese prepared to crush the demonstration with military force, His Holiness made the difficult decision to accept his ministers' advice to take refuge in India. Dressed as an ordinary peasant, the Dalai Lama left the Norbulingka summer palace on horseback on March 17, and was welcomed in Mussoorie by the Indian government on April 20, 1959.

China swiftly responded to the March 10 uprising; by the year's end, eighty-seven thousand Tibetans were dead in the Lhasa region alone. Throughout the following decade, during the Cultural Revolution, China attempted to force the

ABOVE: The robe of Kyabje Trijang Rinpoche awaits his return. This respected lama's altar of finely crafted wood is particularly striking. Virtually all Tibetan homes, no matter how humble, contain an altar holding various sacred objects. RIGHT: The Dalai Lama, fourteenth in the lineage of Dalai Lamas, is both a spiritual and political figure. Wearing a yellow ceremonial hat, His Holiness presides over prayers on the rooftop of Namgyal Monastery.

LEFT: Fast footwork and quick thinking are required of the young artist performing as the hero-prince Dawa Sengay in the opera *Sugkyi Nyima*. In recent years, the Tibetan Institute of Performing Arts has adapted several traditional six-hour operas for audiences interested in two-hour concerts. TOP: In his home near the Library of Tibetan Works and Archives, master painter Chating Jamyang Lama creates a scroll painting, or *tangka*, of Shakyamuni Buddha, in strict accordance with traditional aspects of Buddhist art. ABOVE: Master painter Orgyen Tsewang and his apprentice execute a commissioned Wheel of Existence on an outside wall of Dip Tse Chok Ling Monastery. This traditional circular painting represents the cyclic nature of life.

natives of Tibet to accept communism and reject Buddhism, primarily through indoctrination under severe duress, which included systematic destruction of monasteries, nunneries, and vast collections of literature and art. To date, over one million of the total population of six million Tibetans have died as a direct result of Chinese domination. In addition, the depletion and abuse of Tibet's natural resources have added to the overall devastation of the country.

Soon after the Dalai Lama's arrival in India in 1959, it became evident that the period of exile would be prolonged. The Indian government, in cooperation with the Dalai Lama and his advisers, drew up a list of suitable locations for a Tibetan headquarters. Dharamsala was chosen for its agreeable mountain terrain and the convenience of its largely deserted British military town, founded in 1856, at McLeod Ganj.

Within six months of the original exodus, Tibetan refugee camps overflowed in India and surrounding countries. With strong, unprecedented but cautious support from the Indian government, a Tibetan government-in-exile was rapidly established at Dharamsala, to provide support and hope for those who followed the Dalai Lama into exile. At the age of twenty-four, His Holiness the 14th Dalai Lama of Tibet, considered by Tibetan Buddhists to be an emanation of the Buddha of Compassion, proceeded to oversee the needs of eighty-five thousand homeless Tibetans worldwide.

Refugees continue to escape from Tibet at a steady pace. Most attempt to reach Dharamsala before deciding where to settle. The Dalai Lama regularly meets new arrivals and hears their stories within the gates of his private office and residence beside Namgyal Monastery, where his official religious attendants are trained according to Buddhist tradition. Offices down the hill, in the Tibetan Administration complex, provide assistance for the new exiles who generally arrive ill or exhausted, penniless and traumatized.

ABOVE: A tree branch and merry prayer-flag-raisers cross the Lingkor, a circumambulation route named after its counterpart in Tibet's capital city of Lhasa. The Dharamsala trail encircles major religious institutions, including the Dalai Lama's residence. Hundreds of devout Tibetans walk the twenty-minute circuit on a daily basis while reciting prayers. **LEFT:** Himalayan peaks rising above new Indian-owned hotels in McLeod Ganj hold an allure for mountaineers and others seeking respite from the demands of modern life. **BELOW:** A precocious eight-year-old, Tenzin Lobsang was found at age three to be the reincarnation of an abbot from Dakpo Monastery who died in a Chinese prison in Tibet. The boy is in training to one day become an abbot himself.

The Dalai Lama, who identifies himself as "a simple Buddhist monk," promotes self rule for Tibet in world politics, and is firmly committed to the life of his country's rich culture and to the spirit of his people. In 1963 a draft constitution was promulgated, and democratic reforms have gradually been adopted over time. Based in Dharamsala, the Tibetan Administration's numerous governing bodies and departments provide leadership for such activities as income-generating crafts production, quality educational services for all children, and resettlement projects abroad. All are modest by most modern world standards, but given the odds, Dharamsala's continuing accomplishments are monumental.

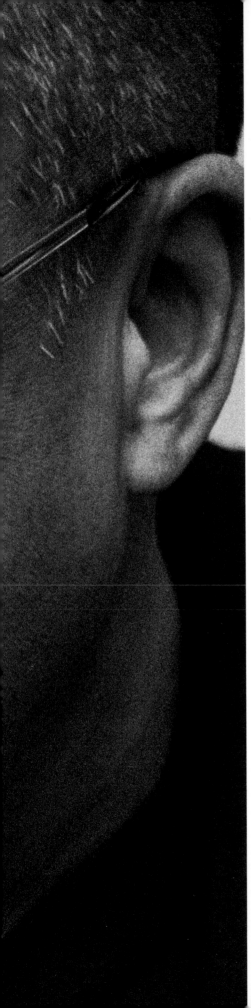

ARMS OF COMPASSION
His Holiness the DALAI LAMA

I t is 9:30 A.M. His Holiness the 14th Dalai Lama of Tibet is seated in the main temple at Thekchen Choeling, the religious complex situated outside the gates of his private residence in Dharamsala, India. Empty mats and pillows, hastily labeled with the names of Western students who have informally reserved seats within view of the highest lama of Tibetan Buddhism, create a patchwork on the courtyard floor.

In the depths of the Central Cathedral at Thekchen Choeling, the Dalai Lama performs private prayers in preparation for the ten days of teachings he will begin later in the day. Apparently, few know of his presence here — His Holiness faces thousands of empty seats in the open temple. The great monk barely moves as he prays. His peace is palpable.

The cathedral's brightly painted upper window frames are designed to be easily removed so that the public may gaze inside. Soon, on this warm, clear Himalayan morning in mid-October, the Dalai Lama will be the focal point for masses of seekers. The Highest Yoga Tantra initiation is scheduled to begin at 1:00 P.M. And although the crowds have not yet arrived, the temple grounds nevertheless stir with a hushed expectancy. Namgyal Monastery ritual attendants scurry about their tasks with a special sense of purpose, while the official interpreter and his assistants silently prepare microphones for the simultaneous English translation. When the teachings begin, those who do not understand Tibetan will tune in to the translated teachings with FM transistor radios.

The Dalai Lama's warmth shines through tinted eyeglasses.

In anticipation of the pressing audience yet to arrive, and always present in the vicinity of His Holiness, alert plainclothes security personnel stand strategically near doors, windows and stairways. A few lay Tibetans stop to prostrate and then gaze affectionately at their exiled national leader, barely noticeable on a dais that faces the huge golden statue of Lord Buddha. There is a serenity here that cannot be so easily felt on other days. A somewhat rare event, the Dalai Lama sits openly in contemplation.

It is 11:00 A.M. Word has spread that His Holiness, regarded by Tibetan Buddhists as an incarnation of the patron deity of Tibet, Chenrezi — the Buddha of Compassion (in Sanskrit, Avalokiteshvara) — is still seated in the Central Cathedral. Numerous Tibetans have gathered to be in his sacred presence. Interested Indian citizens have also arrived, as has a small collection of Europeans and Americans who have found their way to Dharamsala.

Unclaimed spaces for cushions are now scarce, although no one sits yet. The lower windows of the temple remain shut. Individuals stand outside the Central Cathedral, peering in to see the robed figure who looks so small beside the 18-foot statues of Padmasambhava and Chenrezi. The walkway around the cathedral's exterior is filling quickly. The atmosphere is alive with shared excitement and reverence.

11:20 A.M. His Holiness leaves the temple, accompanied by a few monks. He walks slowly, smiling, acknowledging those he passes on the way back to his residence. His warmth radiates in accord with the day's increasing sunshine, and the small crowd becomes extremely quiet. The

Surrounded by well-wishers eager to catch his gaze, the Dalai Lama waits for the driver to maneuver his jeep through the crowd, following an opera presented outdoors by the Tibetan Institute of Performing Arts.

Dalai Lama withdraws. Protective of their reserved places, or eager to find a comfortable spot with even a partial view of the Dalai Lama's raised platform, people move swiftly to claim seats for the upcoming teachings.

11:45 A.M. The crowd has nestled into an ordered arrangement, surrounding the temple with mats on three sides. The elder, most respected masters sit cross-legged on platforms below the Dalai Lama's dais. Other senior lamas are seated on the floor at either side. The majority of Tibetan monks and nuns sit in the temple facing the altar. A few young monks look down on the sanctuary from a room above. Western students who have "sponsored" the religious teachings with monetary support — a long-standing tradition in Tibetan Buddhism — take their assigned places in the heart of the cathedral. And professionals associated with the Tibetan government-in-exile settle near the official interpreter. Stray tourists and Tibetans jostle about, making room for each other.

The hall is filled with the rich gold and maroon robes of the clergy, accented by earthy browns and greens worn by the lay community. The cathedral's glossy yellow pillars and walls are especially noticeable on this bright blue morning, as is the striking series of gaily colored *tangkas* that line the upper walls. The Dalai Lama's dais, now turned to face the congregation, is draped in the five auspicious colors of red, green, yellow, blue, and white. The imposing statue of Lord Buddha gazes serenely from behind.

All lights and butter lamps in the temple have been lit. The metal gates which normally protect the large statues of the Lotus Born Padmasambhava and the thousand-armed Chenrezi have been opened. Elaborate red and white offering cakes, sculpted with care for the occasion, are arranged beside tidy pyramids of fresh fruit in brass bowls. Within the hour, His Holiness the Dalai Lama will return to speak and bestow his blessings.

ABOVE: The Dalai Lama watches the 30th anniversary celebrations at the Tibetan Children's Village from a vantage point above the crowd. RIGHT: Seated on a traditional dais inside the Central Cathedral, the Dalai Lama greets monks from Namgyal Monastery during the "long life" prayer ceremony following his annual 10-day teaching session.

IN HIS PRESENCE

In a circular waiting room attached to the outside gate of the Dalai Lama's residence in Dharamsala — perhaps months after your request for a meeting has been granted — you wait somewhat nervously until a hurried attendant greets you. After passport and belongings

have been checked, you are accompanied up a short hill, paved and surrounded by one of Dharamsala's only cultivated patches of bushes and flowers. You recall that the Dalai Lama enjoys tending plants, and smile at your good fortune in being granted an audience.

A moment later, the attendant escorts you into a second waiting room adorned with decorative tables and a wall of glass cases displaying antiques from Tibet. You're a little closer. Other people, mostly Tibetans on official business, wait their turns to speak privately with the leader of the Tibetan people.

Finally it is time to meet the Dalai Lama. You are escorted outdoors. Surprisingly, His Holiness greets you on the sidewalk, thoroughly happy to see you. Bowing slightly and beaming broadly, the Dalai Lama reaches to take your right hand firmly in both of his. It is as though you are a dear and special friend, someone he has not seen in many years. As you offer him a white silk greeting scarf, or *khata*, he laughingly places it around your neck in return greeting.

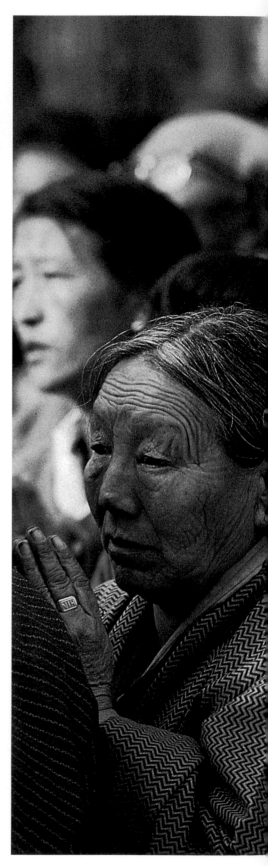

ABOVE: Silhouetted within a spacious tent, the Dalai Lama addresses a gathering above McLeod Ganj. RIGHT: Refugees watch with heightened emotion as the Tibetan flag is raised in Dharamsala on National Uprising Day. Commemorating the demonstrations of 1959, when the people of Lhasa rallied against Chinese rule in Tibet's capital city, March 10 has since been declared a national holiday by the Dalai Lama. Nearly four decades after the takeover, many Tibetans continue to hold the hope that one day Tibet will be free. To prepare for that time, His Holiness has instituted democratic reforms in the Tibetan Administration and has repeatedly attempted to open dialogues with China on the future of Tibet.

You realize that somehow you have entered the Dalai Lama's large meeting room, a space furnished simply and decorated with a few religious paintings. You wonder who will begin. The Dalai Lama waits. This is your interview — it is up to you to set the tone. In fact, His Holiness seems to absorb the mood, responding appropriately to the situation. If you have spiritual or philosophic questions, His Holiness aligns himself as closely as possible with the tradition or background from which you speak. If your focus highlights political or social concerns, his responses mirror your framework.

As usual when the Dalai Lama meets Westerners, an interpeter is present to help clarify words or meanings. The Dalai Lama's English, like his Tibetan, rises and falls in a range of expressive tones, highlighted by his infectious sense of humor.

His voice is calm and penetrating. Scholars say he speaks with incomparable eloquence in the Tibetan language. He delivers Buddhist teachings in his native tongue, but speaks English when he finds it appropriate.

The Dalai Lama nods and listens and smiles, as prominent cheekbones meet the fine network of creases at his shining, penetrating eyes. His unusually glowing skin accentuates a single, inquisitive, v-shaped line that runs the length of his high forehead. Regardless of the topic, brief words of practical advice and grounded viewpoint are woven into a conversation that begins and ends with your own initiative. Tenzin Gyatso is not interested in gaining converts or becoming embroiled in emotion. He is simply there for you, to become engaged in a warm, personal exchange.

You notice, fleetingly, that the Dalai Lama's hands are exquisite. His long, slender fingers close gently around each other as he listens to you speak. Suddenly his hands open wide, then pull together in a hollow clap as he breaks forth into laughter. When talking, the fingertips of one hand rest lightly against those of the other, or the wrists subtly rotate to open the palms outward into heartfelt gestures created by gracefully curved fingers. His Holiness seems to naturally incorporate the spiritual quality of ancient religious Tibetan dance into his daily life. There is a weightless, artistic expression in the Dalai Lama's hands, as multifaceted as the thousand arms of the compassionate Buddha he is said to embody.

ABOVE: Welcoming the New Year, monks, lamas and dignitaries join the Dalai Lama in prayer on the Central Cathedral rooftop. RIGHT: A sacred Buddhist image wrapped in a white silk greeting scarf is presented to the Dalai Lama by a refugee. His Holiness tries to meet the many exiles who arrive in Dharamsala after dangerous journeys through the Himalaya mountains.

Most significantly, the Dalai Lama loves to laugh. Whether in rippling giggles or a clear, open gale, his sense of joy pervades his entire being. While he may roar briefly in response to something you have said, never do you feel ridiculed, for Tenzin Gyatso is laughing beyond personal psychology or irony. And his outburst is generally accompanied by a comment that clarifies the deep level of his humor. His is an unaffected, unselfconscious mirth; he seems to be the Enlightened One smitten with the glory of being alive. Suddenly, your concerns, your doubts, your preoccupations vanish in the presence of this bright-eyed Tibetan monk.

You are not abruptly told to leave, but gradually you come to know that your audience with the Dalai Lama has ended. His Holiness walks you to the door and even escorts you outside, all the time chuckling and bowing to you with great pleasure. You feel he is sincerely glad to have met you. As the next visitor from the waiting room passes you to meet the Dalai Lama, you find yourself bowing and giggling like Tenzin Gyatso himself. Finally, you bound down the mountainside with new grace — enamored, uplifted, mystified and inspired.

DAILY LIFE IN EXILE

As a monk who is both publicly active and contemplative, the Dalai Lama keeps strict, self-imposed monastic vows. He wakes at four in the morning and dedicates his day to others as he recites sacred scriptures. He meditates until 5:30 A.M., after which he performs a series of

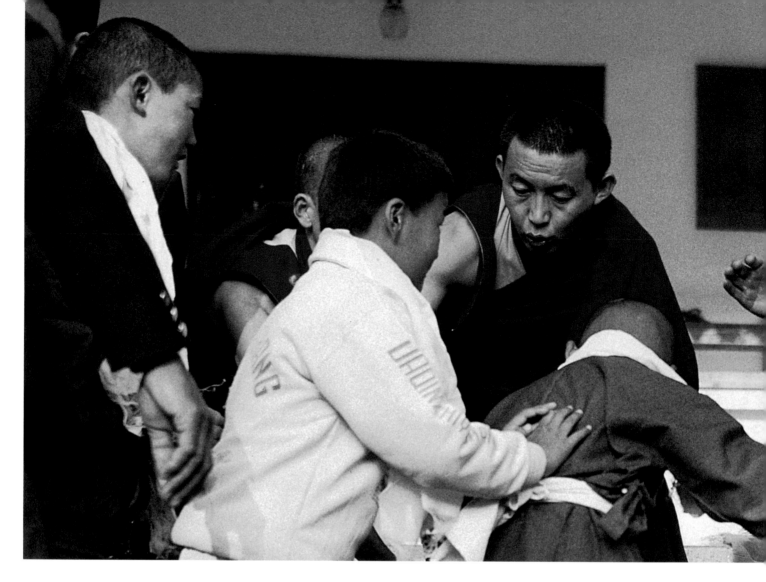

prostrations, practices a Buddhist confession, and recites more prayers devoted to the welfare of all living creatures. After a stroll in his garden and a simple breakfast taken while listening to world news on the radio, the Dalai Lama meditates until nine. Then he reads — everything from Tibetan religious texts to the latest advancements in Western physics and neurobiology. He takes breaks by indulging in his favorite hobby — repairing mechanical devices, particularly watches. All this before his 12:30 lunch!

The Tibetan head of state generally spends afternoons with cabinet members and other government representatives, religious leaders and recent refugees. Throughout the day, the Dalai Lama meditates numerous times. At six in the evening His Holiness relaxes with tea, his last sustenance until the next morning. As a monk, he does not eat dinner. At seven the Dalai Lama watches television — if there is an interesting broadcast in English.

Before going to bed at about 9:00 P.M., His Holiness again prays and meditates. His role in exile is in keeping with his more traditional role as the Buddha of Compassion, who appears in Tibetan iconography with four, eleven, or a thousand giving arms. Where death, repression and displacement threaten his people, this dynamic leader radiates optimism, hope and charity.

THE DALAI LAMA'S EARLY LIFE

From his earliest youth, His Holiness has been recognized as exceptional. Certain auspicious signs were noted on the day of his birth on July 6, 1935, in the village of Taktser, Tibet. And in 1937, high lamas and Tibetan officials were led by premonitions and divinations to the 2-year-old Lhamo Dhondrub.

Disguising themselves as merchants, members of the search party tested the child by asking him to identify the previous Dalai Lama's belongings and answer a series of

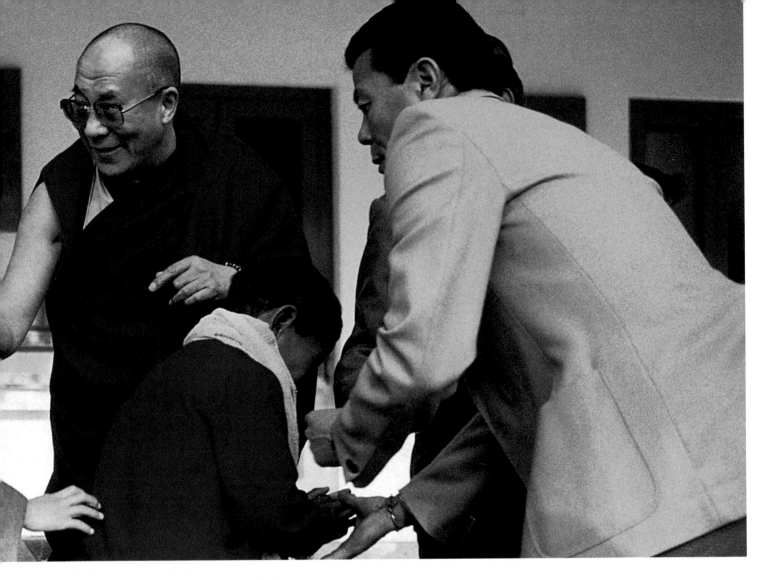

TOP: Tibetan children receive the Dalai Lama's blessings as they are moved through a reception line by attendants. His Holiness places a priority on contact with youth in exile, regarding the welfare of children as essential to the continuation of Tibetan cultural identity. ABOVE: Wrapped in ritual robes and in deep concentration, the Dalai Lama chants during a break in his annual Dharamsala teachings.

questions. In addition to his successful responses, the child innocently offered further information, convincing the officials they had found the next successor to the Lion Throne, a position earned through rebirth rather than inheritance.

In August 1939, a delegation took the boy and his family on the 2-month journey to the Tibetan capital of Lhasa. Their destination was the magnificent Potala Palace. Another two months later, the child took his novice vows. Before reaching the age of 5, the youngster was installed — pending reaching the age of maturity — as the 14th Dalai Lama of Tibet. His name was now Tenzin Gyatso, or Ocean of Wisdom, shortened from Jetsun Jampel Ngawang Lobsang Yeshi Tenzin Gyatso.

At age 6, the young Dalai Lama began an 18-year course of studies with primary emphasis on Buddhist metaphysics and philosophic debate. Tenzin Gyatso spent the winter months at the Potala Palace. For the summer seasons, he traveled two miles west to enjoy country life at the Norbulingka, or Jewel Park. Here, he taught himself to disassemble

LEFT: With Tibetan lamas and Jewish leaders looking on, the Dalai Lama laughs as Rabbi Zalman Schacter-Shalomi recites a humorous poem during a 1990 conference. His Holiness has a particular interest in the challenges faced by each of history's exiled or threatened peoples. FAR LEFT: A majestic Buddha sits behind the Dalai Lama, who wears a participant's identification badge on his robes during a 1990 Mind/Life conference. Focusing on the connection between Tibetan Buddhism and modern psychology, the event is one of many supported by the Dalai Lama, who encourages ongoing dialogue between scholars of Buddhism and the sciences.

and reconstruct the few mechanical items in Tibet at that time. He was also interested in geography and Western civilization, virtually unknown subjects in isolated Tibet.

On January 1, 1950, Radio Peking announced the intention of the People's Liberation Army to "liberate Tibet," along with Taiwan and Hainan. Chinese troops had already begun to infiltrate Tibet. On October 25, China finally announced that troops were in the process of defeating "imperialist oppression" in that country. The Dalai Lama was only 15, three years younger than the accepted age for ascending the throne. But the Chinese were at hand and Tibet needed a ruler. The medium of the Gadong State Oracle was summoned by advisers. Standing before the teenager, the Oracle insisted, "Make him king!" In November, Tenzin Gyatso was installed as Tibet's active temporal leader. Throughout the next nine years, the Dalai Lama spent his time studying for his Doctor of Divinity, or Geshe Lharampa degree, while working to keep peace between the Tibetan people and the Chinese army.

At the age of 24, the Dalai Lama sat for his final examinations at Lhasa's Jokhang Temple. Eighty scholars questioned the young man all day and well into the night as 20,000 monks watched and listened. Tibet's most respected scholars and abbots agreed that the young Tenzin Gyatso's

abilities were unusual, even phenomenal. This was early March, 1959. Within two weeks, tensions in the capital had reached a crisis as thousands of Tibetans surrounded his residence at the summer palace; Chinese military police angrily insisted he turn himself over to their "protection." It was decided that the Dalai Lama's life was in danger and the young leader could best serve his people by fleeing Tibet. Shortly after his secret departure, the Chinese began shelling the Norbulingka and machine-gunning the citizens who had turned out to defend their leader. With the Dalai Lama gone, communist leaders dissolved the Tibetan Administration. The Dalai Lama, however, promptly announced his formation of a government-in-exile.

Thirty years later, the Dalai Lama was awarded the Nobel Peace Prize. He speaks of the late Indian pacifist Mahatma Gandhi as an inspiration. The Dalai Lama understands the motivation behind violence but does not accept its use. He fosters pride in Tibetan identity and discourages animosity toward the Chinese. He encourages his people to persevere in the face of grave sorrow and near extinction. He teaches universal compassion and lives its precepts. Due to the Dalai Lama's foresight and direct guidance, the rich culture of Tibet still thrives. Rarely in history have political and spiritual leadership been so uniquely balanced.

SECURITY AND SCHOLARSHIP
Tibetan
Children's Village

The Tibetan Children's Village, a sprawling 43-acre community situated on a tree-ringed plateau above McLeod Ganj, is a city in itself. The residential facility for children houses one-third of Dharamsala's Tibetan population. The young people here hold the hope of a continued collective Tibetan identity and are raised to respect their heritage. Equipped with many specialized facilities, including an unusual cluster of octagonal, dome-roofed structures, the Tibetan Children's Village (TCV) meets the needs of 2,000 residents, most of whom are orphans or youngsters whose surviving parents are unable to care for them.

Like their elders, Tibetan children are openly affectionate, clasping each other about the shoulders when walking across the grounds, or spontaneously holding hands when talking. Teenagers can be seen rehearsing a student-written play or working on chemistry projects together while younger boys and girls jump rope, play soccer or weave colorful cloth bracelets for each other. In a quiet room nearby, a middle-aged woman tenderly cuddles and feeds an infant whose mother did not survive the harsh journey from Tibet to India.

During the massive exodus from Tibet in 1959, thousands of sick and abandoned children wandered through refugee camps, separated from their families either by death or the chaos of displacement. The Dalai Lama noted the devastating effects of exile on young children and decided to establish a center to care for destitute youngsters. In 1960, a group of fifty-one starving children, initially tended by members of His Holiness' own entourage, was brought from Jammu, North India, to join the newly formed community of Tibetans in Dharamsala.

As word of Dharamsala's refugee nursery spread into Tibet, an underground network was established to safely smuggle children into India for protection against communist indoctrination and neglect by Chinese oppressors. International interest was sparked — food, clothing, medical supplies, and funds for school and housing construction poured into the refugee community to aid the children of Tibet.

High school students at the Tibetan Children's Village (TCV) participate in the school's 30th anniversary celebration, where the Tibetan national flag, banned in Tibet by the People's Republic of China, is proudly displayed.

Dharamsala's initial group of youngsters was supervised by Tsering Dolma Takla, the Dalai Lama's elder sister, founder and director of the early Nursery for Tibetan Refugee Children. She was later succeeded by their younger sister, Pema Gyalpo, who subsequently founded the Tibetan Children's Village and continues to serve as its director. Fondly known as Jetsun Pema, TCV's director is an energetic and efficient leader, pivotal in the recent establishment of branch villages, day schools, old people's homes, and health care centers in both India and Ladakh.

At first, each youngster was fed, clothed, and given medical treatment. At eight years of age, children were sent to neighboring residential schools. Within its first 10 years, more than 3,500 children had received care at the nursery. Eventually, vacancies no longer existed in the local schools. It became clear that a new plan was needed. In 1972 the Tibetan Children's Village was formally registered as a member of SOS Kinderdorf International, the organizing body that has inspired establishment of SOS Children's Villages worldwide. This affiliation solidified TCV's status as a fully integrated community, providing complete living and educational environments in one setting. Several children's villages were later established at other Tibetan refugee settlements, and in 1984 Dharamsala's second children's village was built below the Kotwali Bazaar.

At TCV, Tibetan ideals are blended with progressive scholarship in a balanced, forward-thinking system of education. English is the medium of instruction for older students. Teachers, most of whom attended TCV schools themselves, weave Tibetan folk tales, history, and religion into the curriculum. A love for the dignity of the endangered culture of the homeland is reinforced, and a future in liberated Tibet is embraced as the common goal.

In the living environment, each child belongs to a "home" where two foster parents look after the needs of about 35 students. Generally, one designated parent takes care of the "family" while the partner works as a TCV teacher, secretary, carpenter, shopkeeper, driver, or in another trade crucial to the success of the village. The various age groups support and care for each other as in a traditional family. Each home is issued a gas stove for cooking, so children can eat in a family setting rather than a mess hall. Caretakers receive instruction in nutrition and health, and medical care is organized under the auspices of one of the village's twelve committees.

To prepare students for entrance into the modern world's work force, Tibetan Children's Village schools have adopted English as the primary language of instruction.

When compared with the earlier influx of children at the beginning of the Tibetan diaspora, not as many orphans now seek admission to Dharamsala's children's village and its affiliates. However, youngsters in economic need receive primary consideration for acceptance. Seventy-five percent of those admitted are destitute. Ten percent are children of Tibetan Administration officials who earn low wages and contribute minimal fees. The remaining fifteen percent come from families who pay full tuition. Otherwise, children younger than the age of six are generally not accepted if both parents or a single mother are alive and able to raise the child.

By all outer appearances, the Tibetan Children's Village is affluent. Its stunning location and attractive buildings belie the fact that TCV depends upon the generosity of philanthropic organizations and individuals. Most contributions come through international support efforts that match needy Tibetan children with individual sponsors or specific programs. But in each location, the children's villages work toward self-sufficiency. In Dharamsala, TCV's handicraft/vocational center, established to train young people in the traditional arts of Tibet, is proving itself financially viable while contributing to the survival of Tibetan culture.

LEFT: An outdoor breakfast is enjoyed by elementary school children at TCV, a resident community. Most of the children are either orphans or unable to be fully supported by living parents. Other youngsters are sent to TCV by parents seeking an education that includes instruction in Tibetan history and culture. TOP RIGHT: Colorful flash cards assist a small child learning to read. ABOVE LEFT: TCV teachers, many themselves graduates of TCV schools, have a special empathy for children raised in exile. ABOVE RIGHT: A little girl finds the quickest way to quench her thirst at a communal water spout outside the Tibetan Children's Village day school in McLeod Ganj. NEXT PAGE: In a well-rehearsed pageant during TCV's 30th anniversary commemoration in 1990, high school students form an "endless knot," the ancient Tibetan symbol of good fortune.

BALANCED SPIRITUALITY
Namgyal Monastery

As streaks of orange tinge the sky at dusk, dozens of Namgyal Monastery monks stroll onto the Thekchen Choeling courtyard below the main temple. Laughing and gently nudging each other, the robed figures informally take their places on a long, wide platform. They sit in a circle to recite a prayer in unison before breaking animatedly into groups. Soon the courtyard reverberates with a din of clapping, stomping, and rapidly escalating exclamations. What may appear to be a game or dance is actually a philosophic debate, integral to activities at the Dalai Lama's private monastery, and an intellectual challenge clearly enjoyed by many Tibetan monastics. The debates continue as the Himalayan sky darkens into night.

Hours before the shops of McLeod Ganj open the following morning, paths from the town to the temple begin to fill with Tibetans turning strings of prayer beads between their fingers while reciting sacred phrases, *mantra*, as they stroll towards Namgyal Monastery for early devotions. Several lay persons practice repeated prostrations

outside the temple's entrance, sliding their hands onto the concrete floor with the assistance of small cloth pads. Others spin tall metal prayer wheels attached to the outside walls of the building, walking in clockwise circumambulations around the temple. Throughout each day, the temple and its courtyard resonate with activity. Unquestionably, this site is the hub of religious activity in Dharamsala.

The Namgyal Monastery office, displaying one of Dharamsala's few signs written in English, is often a traveler's first stop upon arrival here. It sits at the top of the steeply winding incline connecting the Tibetan Administration complex to the village of McLeod Ganj. Adjacent to the

ABOVE: A Namgyal monk applies finishing touches to a butter sculpture for the Tibetan New Year. RIGHT: Seated at the entrance to the Central Cathedral during New Year celebrations, monks from Namgyal Monastery perform special hand gestures while chanting. Each detail of the robes and head-dresses is symbolic of a specific aspect of Tibetan Buddhist philosophy.

School of Buddhist Dialectics, the monastery is responsible for maintaining important ritual practices and taking a nonsectarian approach to teachings from each lineage of Tibetan Buddhism.

More than two hundred monks pursue the traditional course of studies at Namgyal Monastery. Success in meditative equilibrium, the refinement of philosophic inquiry, and perfection of the sacred religious arts (such as sand mandala construction and ritual music and dance performance), are goals that serve as foundations for the monastic education. A majority of the monks at Namgyal eventually earn a degree called Master of Sutra and Tantra. Some continue their studies to earn the highest scholastic degree, Geshe, which generally takes about twenty years to complete.

Namgyal Monastery has worked closely with each Dalai Lama since the institution was founded in Tibet's capital city, Lhasa, by the Second Dalai Lama in the 16th century. Following the Chinese invasion of Tibet and the 1959 popular uprising, Namgyal monks who had fled their homeland lived in a small house outside Dharamsala until the present Dalai Lama reestablished the monastery at its current location alongside his own private residence.

Panoramic views of the spectacular peaks and sprawling valley make the monastery's location perfect for contemplation and religious aspiration. In old Tibet, monasteries proliferated as community focal points, just as they now do in exile. The fellowship of monks is one of close, lighthearted interaction, defying Western notions of staid solemnity. Most families encourage at least one child to join a monastery or nunnery, especially if that child proves to be the reincarnation of a respected spiritual master, or *tulku*. Children living in monasteries are treated with great affection, receive an excellent education, and are protected by the monastic community. Their masters humbly acknowledge their own status as precious holders of a great tradition; through them, younger Tibetans and other serious students will bring new life to one of the world's oldest and most complete systems of religious philosophy.

FAR LEFT: With noses and mouths covered to symbolically prevent impurities from being breathed onto the sacred space, Namgyal monks make preparations for a fire ceremony. TOP LEFT: Denma Locho Rinpoche, then abbot of the Namgyal Monastery, relaxes in his room. LEFT: Uninhibited during the sedate proceedings taking place in the temple, young Tenzin Lobsang plays with a plastic ball. One of just a few children residing at the monastery, the boy is an officially recognized reincarnate lama, or *tulku*.

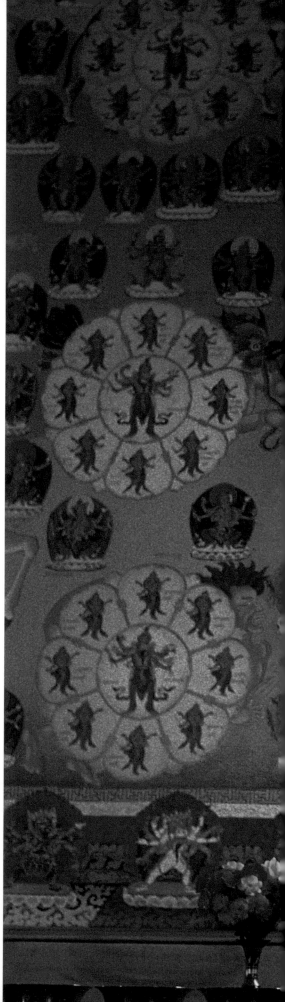

PREVIOUS PAGE: Scores of Namgyal Monastery monks gather beneath paintings adorning the Central Cathedral at Thekchen Choeling to receive teachings from the Dalai Lama, seated on a dais at the altar. As monks of the Dalai Lama's personal monastery, Namgyal monks consider themselves fortunate to have regular contact with the highest lama in Tibetan Buddhism. ABOVE: A large Kalachakra mandala dominates the west wall of the Kalachakra temple of Namgyal Monastery. Mural paintings for the new temple were completed in 1993. RIGHT: The altar of the Namgyal Kalachakra temple includes a striking fresco, with Shakyamuni Buddha at the center. NEXT PAGE: Enjoying the challenge, Namgyal monks participate in a debate class held in front of the monastery's library. During the traditional dialectic matches, a standing monk enthusiastically poses philosophic questions to a seated monk, who must rapidly defend his viewpoint. Standard hand and foot gestures are utilized in debates, making sessions look somewhat like theatrical presentations.

만다라

Student dancers nervously sneak a glance while a fellow monk takes a Kalachakra ritual dance examination. Sacred dance, one of several art forms considered integral to tantric Tibetan Buddhism, is generally performed only by specially trained monastics and contains symbolism that is regarded as spiritually potent for both practitioner and observer.

ABOVE: Khamtrul Rinpoche, the highly respected Nyingma master appointed by the Dalai Lama to oversee certain tantric practices at Namgyal Monastery, is considered an expert in each of the sacred arts of Tibet.
RIGHT: Required to perform a randomly selected portion of the lengthy Kalachakra dance text, a young monk is examined by three senior monks in a monastery classroom. Ngawang Topgyal, far left, trained 30 monks daily for two months; only five were eventually selected to perform during public teachings given by the Dalai Lama.

BUDDHAS, DAKINIS, PRIMARY COLORS
Visual Arts and Handicrafts

McLeod Ganj has the look of an early American frontier town. But behind the rustic shops and simple homes thrives a richly textured network of artistic enterprise. The visual arts of Tibet are almost exclusively religious in nature; major art forms are based on adherence to strict guidelines described in sacred texts. In essence, each piece serves a ritual function or enhances the practice of meditation.

Precisely crafted religious scroll paintings, called *tangkas*, depict brightly colored iconographic figures such as peaceful buddhas, lovely "sky beings" called *dakinis*, or fierce deities residing in their respective fiery realms or glorious heavens. Artists are not only technically trained to produce meticulously detailed works, but are also taught by their masters to actively seek spiritual calm and moral fortitude. As part of this process, *tangka* painters traditionally observe dietary and hygienic disciplines while in the process of creating. In Dharamsala, young artists selected through a program sponsored by the Tibetan Administration study for at least 10 years in a window-lined studio beside the Library of Tibetan Works and Archives. Independent artists, some associated with Tibetan Children's Village handicraft centers, are commissioned to create *tangkas* for families or monasteries, or to execute paintings on temple walls.

In a room adjacent to the painting studio, woodworking students are trained to carve intricate patterns for altars, decorative furniture and architectural detailing. Woodworkers are generally permitted more creative expression than *tangka* painters, as their designs are less strictly religious in nature. Delicate carvings of birds, flowers, foliage, trees, small animals, and mythological figures are elegantly interwoven into stunning designs.

In his one-room home and studio at the Nyingma monastery Zilnon Kagye Ling, master sculptor Kalsang Dorje paints one of the statues commissioned by the Dalai Lama for temples in exile.

Metalwork, primarily in brass, is an important craft. Craftspersons principally produce ritual implements and metal statues of the Buddha in various forms. Metalwork in the Tibetan tradition is a discipline whereby teachers directly impart the technique to students, without the written guidelines found in other art forms. Thus, a close relationship between master and apprentice must be cultivated for the art to survive.

In Tibet, before the diaspora, artists specialized in one traditional art form. Now, in exile, they often study several mediums, sometimes settling for whatever instruction they can find or for an art form that might provide a more practical livelihood. Fiberglass

mask-making, for example, has evolved as an inexpensive alternative to clay products made only by specially trained masters. On the other hand, certain skills are not altered. Tibetan sand painting, a painstaking process involving the scraping of colored sand from a funnel into symbolic circular designs called *mandalas*, continues to be taught exclusively in monastic settings and is a highly specialized religious art.

Tibetan carpet weaving is a cottage industry supported widely by the Tibetan Administration. Providing income for a large population of Tibetan workers, carpet production is an indigenous Tibetan art that has proven profitable. The brightly hued carpets, with their swirling details and symbolic designs, were used in Tibet as horse blankets and warm, decorative coverings for couches. Now, in exile, carpets are still used as couch covers. Foreigners are more fond than Tibetans of using them to decorate floors or to display as wall hangings. Carpets in a vast array of sizes and designs, both traditional and contemporary, can be purchased and shipped overseas at a savings.

In addition to items actually made in the region, shops carry a wide assortment of handicrafts produced throughout India, Nepal, and Ladakh. Jewelry, crafted mainly in silver and adorned with turquoise or coral, is inexpensive and generally well-made. Tibetan bowls, bells, and other household or ritual objects are always in demand, while handmade novelty items, such as attractive backpacks claimed to be woven from yak hair, appear for a while and are soon replaced by a new line of crafts.

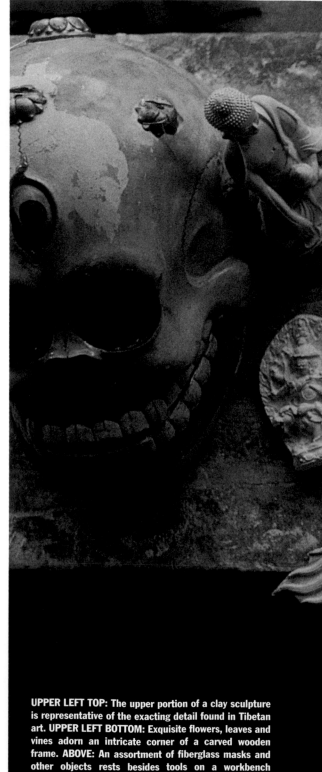

UPPER LEFT TOP: The upper portion of a clay sculpture is representative of the exacting detail found in Tibetan art. UPPER LEFT BOTTOM: Exquisite flowers, leaves and vines adorn an intricate corner of a carved wooden frame. ABOVE: An assortment of fiberglass masks and other objects rests besides tools on a workbench at a handicraft center in Dharamsala. The Tibetan Administration supports artistic enterprises to preserve Tibet's rich cultural heritage and to train exiles for future employment.

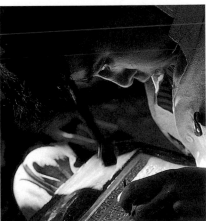

LEFT: A young mother working at a carpet weaving center near the Library of Tibetan Works and Archives provides financial support for her family. The carpets have become popular in Western countries and are a major source of income for Tibetan refugees. TOP: Colorful carpets are frequently seen drying on balconies in the exile community. ABOVE LEFT: The late Rigzin Paljor puts finishing touches on a *tangka* painting. The traditionally detailed scroll painting is executed on canvas stretched in a wooden frame, and will later be mounted on a multi-colored brocade background. ABOVE CENTER: Rolls of colored yarn to be used in carpet manufacture hang in the handicraft center. Artisans specialize in various aspects of carpet production, from dyeing and rolling the hand-spun yarn, to weaving, sculpting, trimming and selling the entirely handmade product. ABOVE RIGHT: Metalwork is a less commonly practiced art, especially since there are fewer skilled masters, and materials are scarce in exile.

FAR LEFT: A young Tibetan student at the Norbulingka's Center for the Arts copies a drawing of a deity. Proportions for these figures, fixed by tradition, are indicated by grid lines. ABOVE: Students at Dip Tse Chok Ling Monastery practice for an upcoming mandala examination by scraping colored grains of sand through a funnel onto a platform. Each aspect of mandala construction follows strict requirements, said to be inspired by the meditative experiences and dreams of sages. CENTER: A delicate sand painting, approximately seven feet in diameter, will be swept together and scattered at the conclusion of religious practices associated with the deity Vajrabhairava. Each element of the complex design holds a symbolic meaning specific to this deity. BOTTOM: A Namgyal Monastery monk, with painstaking care, pours colored grains of sand through a funnel onto a platform. Artists begin the process by marking the work area with architectural lines in white chalk, and then apply sand from the center outwards.

The Library Complex

THE TIBETAN ADMINISTRATION

D haramsala's taxi drivers conveniently refer to it as "the Library," and indeed the Library of Tibetan Works and Archives is located within the security of its walls. But the Tibetan Administration compound contains much more. Each morning, dozens of professionals walk their young children to school before entering the government-in-exile courtyard through a colorful Tibetan-style gate.

Situated at a comparatively level juncture between lower Dharamsala and McLeod Ganj, the Tibetan Administration sits in a natural cradle which overlooks the sprawling Kangra Valley and gazes upward into the majestic Dhauladur mountain range. It is the starting point for myriad Tibetan activities worldwide. The atmosphere here is at once businesslike and casual; the communal spirit is strong. Large thermoses of hot tea are brought from home each morning to offices nestled together in the Administration complex. Deadlines are loosely projected goals, met with little of the harried stress familiar to the Western world.

Simple daily lunches are provided for all employees. Tibetan Administration offices empty quickly when a paunchy, t-shirt clad cook stands on a rooftop and repeatedly strikes a hand-held gong to announce mealtime. In a facility reminiscent of a mess hall at an American summer camp, affectionate friends exchange light banter. Several times a year the Tibetan Administration sponsors special events for family members. The mood is more like a village picnic than an official gathering.

The Tibetan Administration has been developing a democratic system of government since 1963, when His Holiness the Dalai Lama presented a draft constitution for approval by the refugee population. Where formerly, in Tibet, government officials were appointed by the Dalai Lama, most are now elected to office. For a people who continue to believe wholeheartedly in the judgment of each incoming Dalai Lama, traditionally accepted as the spiritual and political leader of Tibet, this transition to democracy has not been easy, especially during the tenuous and prolonged period of upheaval and relocation. But common goals and firm resolve pervade government-in-exile endeavors. Staff members know that Tibetan cultural identity is, in a very real sense, in their hands.

The Kashag, or cabinet, is the government-in-exile's highest executive body. Its members work closely with the Dalai Lama. In 1991 (the International Year of Tibet), the first elected Kashag was installed by the administration. Each department of the Tibetan Administration, also known as the Central Tibetan Secretariat, is responsible for the daily operation of wide-ranging programs. The Office of Information and International Relations, and the Council for Religious and Cultural Affairs, are the most visible. The first acts as an information outlet, disseminating continually updated facts on Tibetan issues to news sources and governments.

The doorway to the Library of Tibetan Works and Archives welcomes visitors to a vast collection of historical material.

The second encourages the preservation of Tibetan culture and is particularly active in supporting Buddhist learning.

Other government-in-exile departments administer refugee settlements, oversee the operation of schools and hospitals, assess ongoing needs, and provide housing and other forms of public assistance. The Tibetan Women's Association, although not an official department, works cooperatively with the Tibetan Administration to promulgate and assist with a wide range of efforts. Long days are spent in quietly carrying out diverse projects, such as the distribution of donated clothing and blankets to the needy,

or in determining which children or elderly persons may have special needs.

LIBRARY OF TIBETAN WORKS AND ARCHIVES

Early each morning, Tibetan pilgrims reverently circum-ambulate the Library of Tibetan Works and Archives and prostrate repeatedly in front of its red doors. Westerners soon gather on the front porch, strikingly rich in its brightly detailed Tibetan architectural facade, prior to a philosophy class. An Indian fruit seller arranges his basket and scales for a day of trade.

As a major program of the Tibetan Administration, the Library of Tibetan Works and Archives, completed in 1971, acts as a

repository for texts and art objects. Established to encourage the proliferation of Tibetan scholarship in the modern world, the Library now houses more than 4,000 titles for public reference in separate English and Tibetan language rooms. It also has an impressive film documentation department. Most significantly, more than 60,000 rare manuscripts and 800 works of art, all brought secretly from Tibet to India, are displayed or stored in the Library museum. Periodicals, translated texts and commentaries, and other scholarly works previously inaccessible throughout the world are published by the Library and the Council for Religious and Cultural Affairs. Students of Tibetology travel from all parts of the globe to gain access to the

TOP: Members of the first elected cabinet meet privately with the Dalai Lama in 1990. On the couch to his left sits Kalsang Yeshe and Tenzin Tethong. Across from the Dalai Lama is Jetsun Pema, his younger sister. She is the first woman in Tibetan history to serve as a cabinet minister and is Director of the Tibetan Children's Village. PAGE 78, LEFT: Protecting Tibet's heritage, a painted figure tops a column at the Library. PAGE 78, CENTER: Geshe Sonam Rinchen is one of several teachers at the Library, which offers classes in Buddhist philosophy and Tibetan culture. PAGE 78, RIGHT: To distribute blessings to the four directions, a woman spins the large prayer wheel outside the Library of Tibetan Works and Archives. ABOVE LEFT: The Office of Information and International Relations is the official link between the Tibetan Administration and the outside world. ABOVE CENTER: Rare texts, brought to India from Tibet, are stored in a special research room at the Library. ABOVE RIGHT: The Tibetan Administration gate, next to Delek Hospital, welcomes employees and visitors to government-in-exile offices.

Library's collections or to take courses taught in upstairs classrooms by internationally respected scholars at the Centre for Tibetan Studies. Specific courses on classic works by ancient masters, traditional meditation techniques, Tibetan language, or sociological and anthropological aspects of Tibetan culture are offered year-round. Those who use the facilities at the Library of Tibetan Works and Archives range from well-known academicians to free-spirited seekers, all intent on exploring a heritage rich in intellectual and spiritual challenge.

SCHOOLS FOR THE ARTS AND SCIENCES

At the Tibetan Medical and Astrological Institute, on a spacious campus outside the Tibetan Administration complex, young adult refugees gather daily to learn the fundamentals of the healing arts from respected physicians trained in Tibet. Similarly, accomplished artists specializing in opera and folk performance keep their traditions alive by instructing aspiring singers and dancers at the Tibetan Institute of Performing Arts, its campus located on a scenic plateau above McLeod Ganj. At several locations throughout Dharamsala, particularly at the Norbulingka Institute, masters of Tibetan painting, weaving, woodcarving and metalworking guide select students in techniques of the visual art forms indigenous to ancient Tibet. This colorful range of endeavors has been organized cooperatively by the Tibetan Administration to preserve and encourage the advancement of Tibet's cultural heritage. Government-in-exile funding and administrative support ensures continuation of Tibet's threatened arts.

Tibetan monasteries, nunneries, and schools for children are by far the most heavily utilized programs guided by the Tibetan Administration. Religious institutions, which traditionally focus on the sophisticated philosophic thought and disciplined mysticism of Tibetan Buddhism, provide education for those who wish to pursue monastic studies. And in keeping with Tibetan Buddhism's strong emphasis on scholarship, the administration promotes solid education for youth. Primary and secondary schools provide an impressively broad-based, modern learning environment. Students excel in spite of limited technology and materials; many Tibetans are accepted into high-ranking colleges and universities. Motivated by opportunities provided by the Tibetan Administration, refugees are eager to succeed in the modern world.

Gathered in a centralized location above the Kangra Valley, offices of the Tibetan Administration house the government-in-exile for refugees who have fled the Chinese-occupied homeland of Tibet.

KNOWLEDGE, SENSITIVITY
Nuns of Dharamsala

Two young nuns huddle shyly on a stoop beside a popular cafe, delicately covering their mouths with their fingers as they lean toward each other to speak in hushed voices. In the marketplace at McLeod Ganj an older nun sells fragrant round loaves of hearty wheat bread to an Indian shopkeeper, part of her nunnery's efforts at self-sufficiency. At the temple outside the Dalai Lama's private residence, a small group of nuns congregates behind the many rows of monks who have gathered for a special day of prayers and rituals. Barely distinguishable from their male counterparts, the nuns of Tibetan Buddhism wear the maroon robes and shaven heads characteristic of all who have taken monastic vows.

In Tibet prior to 1959, there were more than 19,000 nuns residing in 600 nunneries of varying sizes, giving the Buddhist world its largest population of cloistered nuns. Historically, Tibetan culture has widely supported Buddhist monastic life, making it customary for many women to choose a life of contemplation and devotion — either in private seclusion or as part of a community. Some nuns spend prolonged periods in both settings. Travel on pilgrimage to holy sites, or in search of teachers, is also common for Tibetan women with strong spiritual longings.

Although nuns and monks in the Tibetan tradition theoretically have been treated with equal respect, differences do exist. The number of men who choose monastic life continues to far outweigh that of women — the prestige and special living conditions enjoyed by monks have not been matched in the community of nuns. But it is in exile, with controversial encouragement from the Dalai Lama, that religious and educational opportunities are now encouraged and instituted for Tibetan nuns.

ABOVE: Nuns at Geden Choeling, currently the largest nunnery in exile, read sacred texts during a morning prayer session in the temple. RIGHT: An independent nun for most of her life, Ven. Tashi Sangmo stands near her mud-floored home above the Nyingma temple. In 1991, the aging nun moved to a home for the elderly near the Dalai Lama's residence.

Dharamsala's first nunnery, currently the largest in exile, is the Geden Choeling Nunnery, overlooking the Kangra Valley from a site near the business district in McLeod Ganj. Its simple rooms and modest temple encircle the women's community. Approximately 100 nuns generally live on the grounds. In recent years, however, the facility has filled beyond capacity with refugee nuns from occupied Tibet arriving regularly in Dharamsala. Two hundred made an exodus together in 1990; about 70 women were crowded into a few rented rooms until land was purchased for the construction of a larger nunnery near the Norbulingka Institute for Tibetan Culture.

The daily schedule at Geden Choeling Nunnery begins with early morning chanting at 6:00 A.M., followed by a light breakfast and general chores. Before noon, the nuns join students and teachers from the Buddhist School of Dialectics for classes in philosophic logic and debate. A hearty lunch, the last meal of the day, is enjoyed as a communal event. The nuns then rest until their 2:00 P.M. grammar and reading classes taught by senior nuns. An afternoon tea break is followed by a study period in which prayers and texts are memorized and chanted. Evenings are often devoted to further debate sessions. The day ends at about 9:00 P.M.

Geden Choeling's nuns shoulder all responsibilities for the nunnery's maintenance, from bookkeeping and cooking to construction and renovation. The nuns also respond to the larger community's requests for rituals and prayers at family events or other private situations. Also performed by monks, these traditional practices are regarded as among the most beneficial ways for monastics to be of service.

Dharamsala's other religious center for women is Jamyang Choeling, a non-sectarian institute for about 25 Buddhist women of various nationalities. Nuns from Tibet, Nepal, and other Himalayan border areas study Buddhist philosophy, Tibetan language, meditation, and useful skills such as typing and the English language. Located in a private niche beyond the Bhagsu Hotel, Jamyang Choeling was founded by a Western Buddhist nun of the Tibetan tradition and has a branch institute in Ladakh, a region at the northern border of India with a strong Tibetan presence.

Some of Dharamsala's nuns are not directly associated with a nunnery at all. Rather, these self-determined women live independently, maintaining their vows and inner commitments outside the strictures imposed by a particular institution. Loyal to the teachers who trained them, independent nuns may participate in a nunnery's activities for a time, but eventually move to a secluded spot or another locality.

Tibetan nuns are typically shy when dealing with others, but are often open, witty, willful, affectionate, and self-confident among themselves. Their distinctive presence in Dharamsala, while outwardly modest and retiring, makes a quiet statement about the dedication and inner strength of women in Tibetan culture. Whether giggling like children over small talk, or sharing with acute sadness the trials endured by so many Tibetans under Chinese rule, the new generation of Buddhist nuns has inherited a devotion and depth of character that have only been strengthened by hardship.

ABOVE: Recent arrivals from Tibet take a study break in their quarters at Geden Choeling Nunnery in McLeod Ganj. RIGHT: On the grounds outside the Central Cathedral, nuns wait for the Dalai Lama to arrive. FAR RIGHT: A Tibetan nun and her Indian friend enjoy each others' company.

The Nechung State Oracle

It is early July in Dharamsala. A short, slender monk wearing traditional robes walks slowly toward the Nechung Monastery temple. He is supported on either arm by fellow monks. Above, on the monastery roof, fragrant clouds of juniper-branch incense waft from a large burner near two long-horn players exquisitely framed by the bright Himalayan background. Invited observers watch the scene with mounting interest. Swooning slightly as he walks, the 33-year-old monk is in the early stages of a scheduled trance, not an everyday event in Dharamsala.

Inside the temple, an ornate throne faces a semicircle of monks, devotees, and special guests. The atmosphere is hushed and expectant. Five-year-old Ling Rinpoche, officially declared to be the reincarnation of the Dalai Lama's deceased senior tutor, sits quietly on a dais opposite the altar. The child awaits sacred interaction with a powerful and beneficent oracle appearing through the body of a monk who regularly sacrifices his own identity to become possessed by an ancient deity. Soon the mediumistic monk will become Nechung, protector of the Tibetan nation.

The transformation is disconcerting, even for Tibetans who have grown up with the tradition. Before their eyes, a gentle, self-disciplined, and sane young man is taken deeper into active trance, by stages, with the assistance of his specially trained attendants and the continuous pounding of monastery drums. As the medium is dressed in a multicolored and layered ritual costume, pots of profusely burning incense, suspended from chains to nearly touch the floor, are slowly swung by monks to distribute a pacifying scent. As he more fully enters the trance state, the medium's arms rise from his sides as though unaffected by gravity. A richly decorated silk brocade robe is ritually placed over his shoulders. A circular steel mirror, adorned with amethyst, turquoise, and sacred phrases, hangs over his chest. Flags and banners complete the costume, which weighs 70 pounds without his head-dress. And yet his entire being appears to grow weightless. As if to keep his body from simply floating above the crowd, two attendants stand on either side of the monk to lower the huge, cumbersome 30-pound head-dress onto his head.

Within 30 minutes of his entrance into the red-walled temple, the medium begins hissing, twitching, and yelping as his personal consciousness is lost to the demands of the possessing deity. Swaying and jerking in an unconscious manner, the medium's body follows Nechung's impulses while attendants quickly reach forward to lovingly adjust his ritual robes and the straps of Nechung's three-foot-high crown.

The medium of the Nechung Oracle is a dedicated monk who spends much of each day in prayer and meditation.

Under normal circumstances, these movements would surely snap a person's neck. The event is both inspiring and bizarre; something "other" has entered.

Suddenly Nechung jumps from his throne and brandishes a threatening sword. Observers pull back instinctively, even though the implement is only symbolically associated with destruction — of internal negativities rather than external forms — and is a weapon for penetrating the nature of reality. And the Nechung State Oracle begins to dance. In rhythmic jumps, the deity moves as though his raiment is made of the lightest silk. Running through the temple with remarkable grace, stopping at each statue as though engaged in conversation with it, the oracular deity embodies unencumbered energy. For the time being, no one remembers that a quiet monk, small of stature, is dancing beneath impossibly heavy ornaments. Rather, a powerful entity mesmerizes the crowd.

Awe and devotion envelop the temple throughout this event. Deeply moved, Tibetans observe a mysterious and complex tradition. Oracles not only predict the future but also serve as protectors, or sometimes as healers. In this case, the great divinity Dorje Drakden, a protector of the Dalai Lama, gives guidance through the medium of the Nechung Oracle. It is not the monk himself who possesses oracular powers — he is simply a channel for the entrance of Dorje Drakden. Called *kuten*, literally "physical base," such channels are men or women who exhibit natural tendencies towards mediumism.

Gradually the medium enters a calmer physical state. At this juncture, the true purpose of the trance is realized. The oracle speaks. In a high, strained voice, accompanied by repeated twitches and yelps, the oracle talks through the body of the monk. As Nechung, he delivers political advice and practical guidance in Tibetan language distorted by a continual curling of the tongue in his mouth. Wordless groans made with fluctuating intonations repeatedly interrupt the oracle's speech. Monastery attendants take rapid notation of Nechung's prophetic utterances, largely unintelligible to the untrained. Finally the oracle sits beside little Ling Rinpoche and speaks intimately and at length to the child, who appears unafraid. The boy's attendants, pleased that Nechung is addressing the youthful *tulku*, draw closer to hear the great protector's advice.

Near the end of the trance, a tall Tibetan woman, a recent refugee who has become known for her trance-like behavior, approaches the oracle. With mannerisms similar to his own, she prostrates before Nechung and attempts to engage him in conversation. Her behavior is highly unconventional; observers at trances are traditionally passive and do not seek interaction with the divinity. Uncertain as to the proper response, attendants protectively approach the oracle but do not interfere with the woman's advances. She eventually sits on the floor, at the oracle's feet. As if in a trance that complements his, her body twitches and her voice breaks as she speaks a strange Tibetan. Nechung seems to understand, and a unique communication takes place.

It is unclear when the trance has actually ended. On this occasion, the monk's attendants lead him from the temple while in an altered state similar to earlier stages of the trance. It is not uncommon, however, for the deity to remain long enough to present

Long-horns and drums accompany a morning prayer ceremony at the Nechung Monastery.

a traditionally knotted red protection cord to each of those who stand in line to receive his blessing. Visibly touched by the authenticity of the trance, observers leave the temple emotionally drained, some in quiet tears.

An opportunity to speak with the medium comes four days later, one week after birthday celebrations for the 14th Dalai Lama. Still recuperating from the two trances undertaken within a three-day period earlier in the week, the *kuten* is withdrawn and relaxed. His statements are translated into English by a distinguished young attendant known simply as Karma-la, who works in the monastery's main office.

ABOVE: Ritual objects, arranged for daily prayer, are essential for practices preparing the medium Thubten Ngodrub for his trance states. LEFT: The Nechung Monastery is one of Dharamsala's most impressive examples of Tibetan architecture.

While we speak, a group of senior Nechung Monastery lamas gathers in the quarters of the Nechung medium to recite special prayers in honor of his birthday, their drums and chants reverberating throughout the monastery compound. The medium talks quietly of his position in Tibetan Buddhism. "A *kuten* is never appointed in the ordinary sense," he says of the selection process. The Tibetan mystical training system refrains from cultivating related practices until an individual is officially recognized as the medium who naturally attracts a particular disembodied entity. "It is automatic because no one can choose. And it is not known when the new medium is to be discovered," the young monk explains in his soft-spoken Tibetan. "Usually the signs are not immediate, but the medium has a close karmic relation to the divinity."

When mediumistic tendencies do become evident, a person is watched and guided until the origin of the behavior is determined. "Many tests and investigations must be made by His Holiness the Dalai Lama and by the Tibetan government," says the *kuten*. "No one ever expected me to be the next medium for the Nechung Oracle — certainly I did not know it." Once recognized, a *kuten* is trained to purify the subtle channels of the body in order to be properly prepared for the demands of the trances.

Born in 1957 as Thubten Ngodrub, the current medium of Nechung Monastery is a refugee who fled his home village of Phari, Tibet, with his parents during the Chinese occupation. The family settled in India. In 1971, at the age of 14, Thubten

Ngodrub joined Dharamsala's new Nechung Monastery, where he eventually completed his studies, was appointed the monastery's Master of Rituals, and anticipated a quiet life of anonymity in exile.

In the meantime, the previous Nechung medium, an elderly monk who had served His Holiness the Dalai Lama and the Tibetan government throughout the crucial years of upheaval in Tibet and resettlement in exile, passed away in 1984. Soon after, the Dalai Lama composed prayers for the discovery of a successor, and the Tibetan people waited to see who might eventually replace the thirteenth *kuten* of the Nechung State Oracle. The tradition has been carried out since 1642, at the initiative of the Great Fifth Dalai Lama, for protection of the newly formed central government of Tibet. The oracle continues to advise each of the Dalai Lamas and the Tibetan government on the welfare of the Tibetan people.

At a special ceremony in front of the statue of the Nechung Oracle in Dharamsala, in late March, 1987, the young Thubten Ngodrub fell into a spontaneous trance. The Dalai Lama was immediately informed of the incident by members of the Tibetan cabinet and the Council for Religious and Cultural Affairs. The 30-year-old monk was then invited to the Dalai Lama's residence, where he was instructed to undertake a meditational retreat. Upon its completion, at the Dalai Lama's request, the young monk entered a trance in His Holiness' presence and was tested according to tradition. Following a subsequent public trance and confirmation of his status as a *kuten*, the medium for the Nechung oracle was officially enthroned in an elaborate ceremony in early September, 1987.

Trances tend to follow a similar order of events each time. The twitching and yelping are part of the process of possession. It is as though the entity strains to keep its energy within the confines of a human body. The Nechung State Oracle is one of the two official state oracles of the Tibetan government in Dharamsala. The second is the Gadong State Oracle, whose *kuten* is from a family lineage of lay mediums associated with the nearby Gadong Monastery. There are also unofficial, popularly accepted entities, such as the protectress

Youdonma, believed by many Dharamsala residents to enter the body of a middle-aged woman who lives in a hut above Gadong Monastery. As is true throughout Tibetan Buddhism, each deity has its own traits and responsibilities.

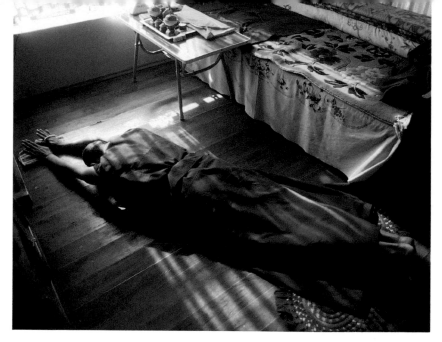

"The whole body serves as a vessel," the Nechung *kuten* says of possession. "The generated wisdom dissolves the usual consciousness until it becomes numb, useless. This is done by the force of the generated wisdom." The medium has no memory of what takes place during trance. Each day his attendants carefully watch his fragile health, as the experience of trance is physically draining.

The Nechung *kuten* conducts two public trances per year, plus several additional trances which are announced to a select circle of individuals a day or two in advance. On some occasions, his ritual dance, said to be the mark of the deity's presence, may be more elaborate than during other trances. "On the whole, this dance is not like the ritual dancing that is commonly practiced by groups of monks in many monasteries," the medium explains. "One cannot rehearse for this."

A *kuten* for the state oracle is in the singular position of being a Buddhist figure who serves, when in trance, as both a political and religious adviser. For all oracles, assisting individuals with their religious lives is a primary responsibility, but with Nechung the guidance is for the people of Tibet via political advice. In contemporary times, Nechung acts as the wrathful defender of the Dalai Lama's peaceful leadership. Special trances are carried out at the Dalai Lama's residence, where Nechung makes ritual offerings to His Holiness before responding to questions posed by the Dalai Lama and members of the government-in-exile. "Even though my position is with the Tibetan government," the *kuten* says, "I do not indulge in the daily work of most officials. My duty is to pray for the government."

Venerable Thubten Ngodrub is an exceptionally sincere young monk who devotes his life to tantric practice. "I used to

ABOVE: Repeated full-length prostrations, part of regular devotions among Tibetans, are practiced faithfully by the medium of the Nechung State Oracle. **RIGHT:** The monk Thubten Ngodrub, who cultivates psychic sensitivity, performs his morning prayers at the Nechung Monastery. Before entering mediumistic trances, attendants dress him in the 70-pound robes and three-foot head-dress associated with the mighty protector deity of Tibet.

study *sutra*," he states, "but I no longer have the disposition for intellectual work." While his status as an important personage may suggest a very public life, the medium actually lives in greater simplicity than many of Dharamsala's respected practitioners. His quarters at the monastery are small and he spends most of his time in quiet seclusion, beginning and ending each day with lengthy prayers. His evening devotions are offerings to the Nechung State Oracle. "I feel my role during those evening times," the *kuten* says gently. "I used to be afraid but I no longer experience that anxiety." In addition to his daily practices, the young monk takes extended devotional retreats a few times a year and receives regular teachings from tantric masters.

The Tibetan medium has been told of the recent interest in channelling that has developed in Western countries. "I do not know much about Western mediums," he admits, "but no one should experiment with this potential. In Tibet, sometimes people will act in a strange manner. They are usually possessed by something, but it is difficult to determine just what. The entity can be the protector of a particular area, or it can be the protector of a child who has just been born. There are purifications that must be done, and there are ways to investigate the matter.

"There is particular danger when someone is possessed by the consciousness of a deceased person. Once attracted to an individual, the entity wants to stay for a long time. It is very dangerous," he warns. "The entity must be exorcised by a highly realized lama. The lama tells the entity to leave for the good of both the spirit itself and the person who is possessed."

Venerable Thubten Ngodrub is hesitant to speak about the young Tibetan woman who apparently had entered a mediumistic trance during his most recent session. "The lamas do not yet know why she was behaving in that way. She has been given spiritual practices to follow and her case will surely be investigated soon."

Visitors to Nechung Monastery, located just below the Library of Tibetan Works and Archives, in the far corner of the Central Tibetan Secretariat complex at Gangchen Kyishong, will see little evidence of its oracular tradition, since its unusual practices are not encouraged as part of daily life. While some of its resident monks will one day become attendants to the Nechung State Oracle and his *kuten*, all are initially schooled with a well-rounded approach to Tibetan Buddhist studies. In fact, this small institution operates much like other Tibetan monasteries, emphasizing study and prayer on a daily basis.

Early each morning chants rise from the Nechung Monastery grounds and into the government offices. In the afternoon, residents spend hours at their studies in the monastery library or classrooms. Physical activities for novices, many between the ages of 12 and 16, range from swimming at a hidden pool in the nearby river, to carrying bricks for a project next door. One would never suspect that here the mighty protector of Tibet prophesies through a sincere and unassuming monk residing within this quiet cloister.

RIGHT: One of a few Nechung Monastery residents literate in the English language, a young student participates in afternoon classes. Religious education takes precedence over other studies in monastic communities. ABOVE: A steady stream of fragrant smoke rises into the clear Himalayan sky while a senior monk adds branches of juniper to the ritual incense stove located on the rooftop of the Nechung Monastery.

YAK DANCES, IRON BRIDGES
Tibetan Institute of Performing Arts

A young man holds an oversized head mask of an animal that looks like a buffalo. Hopping in a caricature of the beast, the dancer's side-to-side antics evoke laughter from observers. Behind him, a second youthful artist follows with the same movements. They are rehearsing a segment from a Tibetan opera. When joined together by a furry black costume, the two performers portray the front and back ends, respectively, of a Tibetan yak.

While a drummer accompanies the yak dancers during their informal outdoor rehearsal, a women's choir is heard from inside a small theatre at the southern end of the horseshoe-shaped compound. Following a morning of individualized instruction, artists at the Tibetan Institute of Performing Arts spend their afternoon preparing the evening's concert. Situated in an isolated niche above the busy town of McLeod Ganj, the institute holds the distinction of being the first organization established in exile for the preservation of Tibetan culture.

The Tibetan Institute of Performing Arts, known simply as "TIPA" by the Dharamsala community, serves as both a live-in school and resident performance company. Young Tibetans gifted in music, dance and drama are accepted as apprentices into TIPA's training program. After several years of academic and artistic schooling, artists may remain as professionals. Some are eventually selected to provide instruction for new students at the institute. Most TIPA graduates move into teaching positions at schools for Tibetan children in exile.

ABOVE: A choir member composes herself before a day-long performance beneath an outdoor canopy. RIGHT: Masked male dancers represent hunters and fishermen who purify the performance space at the beginning of each opera.

Approximately 40 performers work and study at TIPA. Another 40 are costume and instrument builders or administrative and support staff. As with other Tibetan endeavors, a communal spirit connects its members. An overlap of responsibilities is accepted as practical. TIPA's favorite cook, for instance, was once considered a star and is still a highly accomplished senior soloist, best known for his comedic operatic roles.

TIPA specializes in Tibet's two secular forms of theatre: the folk tradition and the operatic repertoire. While Tibetan folk songs and dances are not easy to perfect, it is the multi-faceted opera tradition, *lhamo*, that is particularly challenging for performing artists. Tibetan opera, personally transmitted from master to student without written scores or scripts, was developed by Siddha Tangtong Gyalpo, a 14th-century monk credited with establishing the first Tibetan theatre troupe.

Several versions of Tangtong Gyalpo's life are associated with the introduction of opera into Tibetan culture. In what is perhaps the most historically accurate account, Tangtong Gyalpo shoots a borrowed arrow randomly into the air. It lands in the Kyichu River, an event which he interprets as a directive to build permanent bridges over Tibet's major rivers. In fact, Tangtong Gyalpo became Tibet's inventor of linked chains and designed the first bridges made of iron in Tibet. Culturally, opera became an important link in bridging differences among the geographically dispersed Tibetan people.

Faced with insufficient finances to complete his first major bridge, Tangtong Gyalpo sought a means to find additional support for the project. From among his laborers he selected seven women known for their skills in folk singing and dancing, and rigorously trained them to refine and expand the commonly practiced traditions. Their concerts, accompanied by a single drum and a set of cymbals, became highly popular fund-raising events for the bridge-building enterprise. And Tangtong Gyalpo, one of Tibet's first civil engineers, thus became the country's first stage director.

The mythologized version of Tangtong Gyalpo's life describes the antics of vindictive spirits determined to prevent the completion of his bridges. Each morning laborers awake to find the previous day's work destroyed during the night. Finally, after a long period without progress, the female deity Arya Tara visits Tangtong Gyalpo in a dream and gives him seven links of iron chain. The links immediately turn into seven women dancers who perform flawlessly; their performance is so captivating that the bothersome spirits forget about the bridge. Construction is completed without further interruption.

By the late 15th century, plays with dialogue, music and dance were memorized and enacted for Tibetan New Year festivities. In the 18th century, *Prince Norsang*, written by Rinchen Tsering Wangdu, became the earliest libretto of the *lhamo* repertoire. This first Tibetan opera, adapted from

Members of the Tibetan Institute of Performing Arts' women's choir are dressed as "sky beings," protective feminine entities associated with purified aspects of the human psyche.

stories of the Buddha's previous lives, premiered during the reign of the 7th Dalai Lama. It was during this period that the term *Achi Lhamo*, or Lady Goddess, in honor of the divinity Arya Tara, was first applied to Tibetan theatrical productions.

Tibetan opera soon flowered. Twelve regional performance companies were established. At least fifty new operas were composed, nine of which were gradually accepted as standard classics. The annual Zho Ton, or Great Yogurt Festival, in Lhasa, soon became the focal point for a huge annual *lhamo* competition, held at the culmination of the harvest season. The festival, marked by an ongoing feast of elegant yogurt dishes, gave artists an opportunity to perform before vast audiences. Tibet's four major opera companies vied for popularity, and each year one company was selected as winner of the competition. The grand prize was temporary residency at the Norbulingka, the Dalai Lama's summer palace.

When the communist Chinese crushed the Tibetan uprising in 1959, the performing arts were systematically extinguished except for a few diluted showpieces promoted as tourist attractions by Chinese officials. Fortunately, opera master Ulma Norbu Tsering, once known by his adoring public as Laba, great star of the Kyimulunga troupe from Lhasa, went into exile. Now *lhamo's* only known living master schooled in Tibet, he is responsible for keeping the tradition alive. Daily, Norbu Tsering meets with TIPA's training director and the school's senior dance and music teachers to oversee instruction and rehearsals.

Each Tibetan opera lasts six hours or more and is traditionally presented several times a year in a circular outdoor setting, under a canopy surrounded by an enthusiastic audience of families prepared for a day of merrymaking. Pots of tea and picnic lunches are heartily indulged. Monks and nuns play with small children. Parents and friends gossip during lulls in the program. The performance style is equally casual. But at the arrival of a crucial sequence, familiar to all present, the crowd's full attention focuses on the play. Children and adults openly squeal and laugh

LEFT: A masked dancer in the opera *Pema Woebar* performs for a large audience at the Tibetan Children's Village. In this scene from the opera based on the childhood of the great sage Padmasambhava, a dancing demon is seeking to destroy the good intentions of the young boy destined to spread Buddhism from India to Tibet. ABOVE RIGHT: The only known living opera master trained in Tibet, Norbu Tsering was a major star before the Chinese takeover and now oversees training and direction at the Tibetan Institute of Performing Arts.

when monsters in pajama-like costumes try to scare the crowd; the psychological surrealism of *lhamo* is enhanced by its timeless simplicity.

On May 1, 1984, the Tibetan Institute of Performing Arts' original facility, an old building once used by the British when McLeod Ganj was a hill station, was razed by a devastating fire. All but a few rare antique masks and costumes from Tibet were destroyed. Faced with the ongoing struggles of refugee life, TIPA residents responded with a debilitating sense of defeat, but soon rejoiced when a lucky arrow, uncannily like the one shot by Siddha Tangtong Gyalpo in the 1400's, was discovered intact among charred and scorched ruins. Reconstruction of the institute began almost immediately. And TIPA once again pulsates with the lively music and joy of Tibetan celebration.

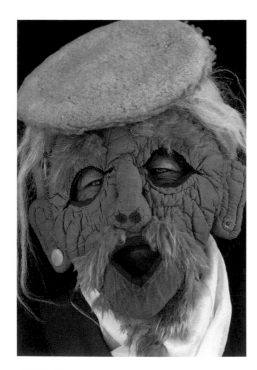

ABOVE: Wearing a unique cloth mask in one of his few select roles, opera master Norbu Tsering continues to appear in productions by the Tibetan Institute of Performing Arts. **RIGHT:** Glaring from their posts on the costume room wall, paper maché masks from the traditional opera *Pema Woebar* are ready to both startle and delight young audiences in Dharamsala.

Touching his own forehead to the head of a visitor in a gesture of mutual respect, five-year-old Ling Rinpoche is already well-versed in the etiquette of giving blessings.

The child Ling Rinpoche and his attendant Lobsang Lungrig have spent lifetimes together. Lungrig was especially close to the late Ling Rinpoche and was instumental in the traditional process of selecting his successor.

Mischievous and intelligent, Ling Rinpoche enjoys playing with toys as much as any other youngster. He is encouraged to develop normally, in spite of his increasingly structured education and responsibilities. LEFT: Pensive, Ling Rinpoche, the child believed to be the reincarnation of the Dalai Lama's late senior tutor, rests briefly between visits from unexpected guests.

CHILD LAMA

Ling Rinpoche

In a sunny clearing at the crest of a tree-lined mountain pathway, a small boy sits in an oversized chair on the veranda of a private cottage. Colorful plastic toys are neatly arranged by an attendant indoors. A monk prepares the child to greet travelers who will offer bananas and mangoes to the youngster, well-trained in the skill of blessing visitors.

This precocious child is the officially confirmed reincarnation of Kyabje Ling Rinpoche, the current Dalai Lama's senior tutor and great friend who died in 1983. Born as Tenzin Chopak in the Tibetan settlement at Bir, the child was discovered at 19 months of age through a traditional process which relies on the proper interpretation of auspicious signs and mystical visions.

As part of his test, the toddler had gathered up his predecessor's prayer beads as if they were his own, then spontaneously offered a tray of sweet biscuits to everyone in the room. This was preceded by a series of divinations performed by the Dalai Lama to determine the child's year of birth and geographic location. Four children showed signs of being the 98th Ganden throne holder. Results of their tests were sent to the Dalai Lama, who then concluded that little Tenzin Chopak was indeed the reincarnation of his beloved former tutor.

As a reincarnate lama, the new Ling Rinpoche has embarked on a lengthy educational journey in which well-rounded excellence is encouraged and nurtured. Already the young child demonstrates mature sensibilities.

He is practically assured of one day holding a high position among Tibetan Buddhist masters. In the meantime, the boy accepts and returns traditional white greeting scarves with an impish grace — and his many visitors leave feeling uplifted and refreshed.

BALANCING THE HUMORS
Tibetan Medical Arts

T ucked in a cranny behind the main row of shops in McLeod Ganj, a small house is pressed between a cramped assortment of shabby structures. Standing in a dark passageway, one wonders if this could possibly be the office of Dr. Yeshe Dhonden, a former personal physician to the Dalai Lama and expert in the ancient science of Tibetan medicine.

Once inside, patients take a numbered metal ticket from an attendant at the front desk and sit on wooden benches in the filled waiting room. Indians, Westerners and Tibetans alike wait patiently for brief sessions with the doctor, well-known for his remarkable skills in diagnosis and cure.

As with other aspects of Tibetan culture, the medical system revolves around the tenets of Tibetan Buddhism. All illness or disease is thought to be indicative of fundamental misconceptions about the true nature of reality. Tibetan medicine

ABOVE: Using three fingers of each hand to diagnose a patient's condition, Dr. Yeshe Dhonden applies gentle pressure for a pulse reading. RIGHT: A Tibetan woman looks to Dr. Yeshe Dhonden for help. Like many who have benefitted by his care, patients attest to the doctor's uncanny healing abilities. According to Dr. Dhonden, "Trans-scientific healing is possible if one practices the teachings of Lord Buddha properly."

seeks a holistic harmony that allows the patient to work with this ignorance and move toward higher levels of understanding.

In the Buddhist worldview, all phenomena exist in dependence on interactions of the five elements — earth, air, fire, water, and space. Tibetan medicine is a complex system which attempts to balance these elements as they operate within the individual. Foods contain myriad combinations of the elements, as do metals, minerals, plants and trees. And emotional states, which affect the three human

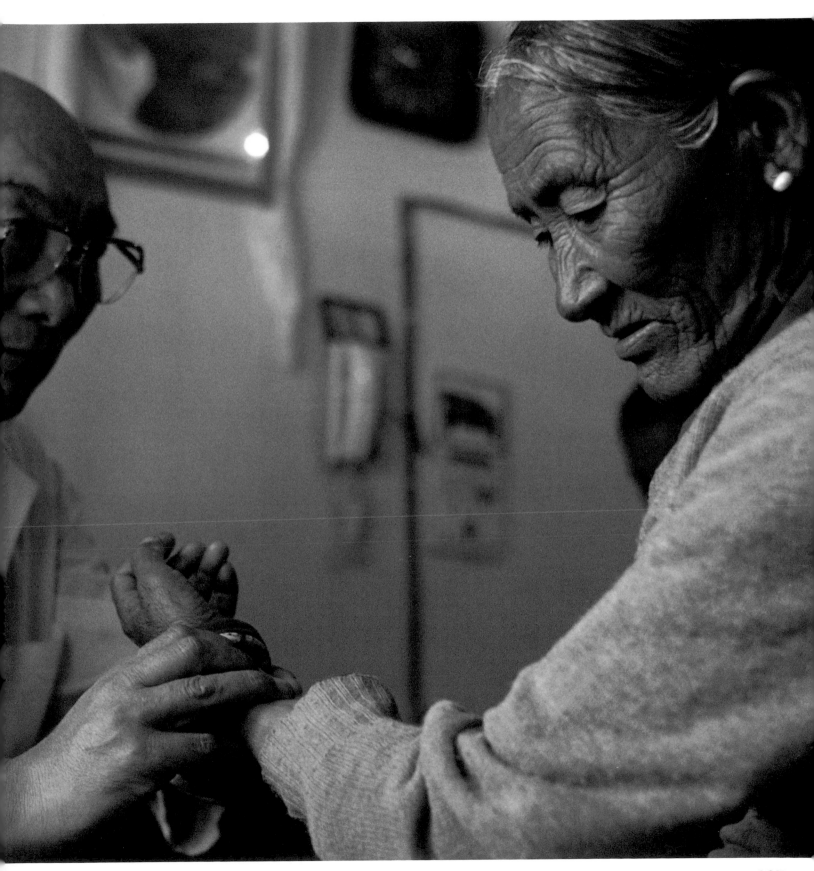

humors — wind, bile and phlegm — are integral considerations in this process. As a result, basic treatments involve a combination of dietary recommendations, the use of medicinal pills, and purposeful shifts in behavior and environment.

In keeping with tradition, a Tibetan physician will maintain inner commitments to live a conscious and disciplined life, not only as an example to patients, but to develop subtle skills for accurate diagnosis and effective treatment. After many years of concentrated study, physicians employ the sophisticated yet seemingly simple art of pulse reading as a primary diagnostic tool.

To begin the evaluation, the doctor reads the pulse by placing his or her middle three fingers on the patient's radial artery. Each finger then exerts a specific pressure. The three fingers of each hand are divided into 12 separations, which correspond to specific organs in the patient's body. To render a meaningful diagnosis, the doctor utilizes considerable tactile and psychic sensitivity.

Dr. Dhonden is not the only physician practicing Tibetan medicine in Dharamsala, although he is perhaps the only private practitioner now in the area. Numerous doctors treat patients at the Tibetan Medical and Astrological Institute, located outside the government-in-exile complex below McLeod Ganj. Dr. Tenzin Chodak, the Dalai Lama's current personal physician, is director of the institute, where he personally trains students in the ancient medical arts of Tibet.

ABOVE: Peeking over the counter at the medicine window in Dr. Yeshe Dhonden's office, a little girl waits for the round, bitter herbal pills that are chewed and swallowed with warm water. **RIGHT:** Large quantities of various herbal pills, manufactured by hand at the Tibetan Medical and Astrological Institute, dry in the sun before being prescribed by trained Tibetan physicians.

THE WEATHERMAN'S MAGIC
Nyingma Monastery

Perched on the edge of a Himalayan cliff, like the monasteries of old Tibet, an isolated cloister is home for a group of long-haired tantric practitioners. Not monastics in the technical sense, the men and women of the Zilnon Kagye Ling temple spend much of each day chanting melodious prayers, live for long periods of time in meditative retreat from the world, and are generally respected for their disciplined commitment to the spiritual life.

This is a temple of the Nyingma lineage, one of the five branches — including the pre-Buddhist heritage — of Tibetan spirituality. All schools seek to balance the various aspects of religious development, yet each of the lineages tends to emphasize a particular aspect of training, its inspiration drawn from approaches taken by early masters and founders of the line. Nyingma practitioners, like those of this small community on the rocky incline above McLeod Ganj, concentrate on the refinement of mystical practice.

Zilnon Kagye Ling was built at the Dalai Lama's request by the late Lama Yeshi Dorje, the tantric "weather controller" who spent more than a decade in solitary retreat in Tibet, becoming a master of the occult arts — including the manipulation of wind, clouds, rain and sun for religious events where vast crowds were expected to gather. A feisty and somewhat irreverent personality, the renowned *nagpa*, or yogi with occult powers, gained rapid respect in exile as a faith healer expert in ancient methods of exorcism. A few years before Lama Yeshi Dorje's death in 1993, he was named *Ngag-jang* (learned *nagpa*) by the Dalai Lama, an honor earned by only a few Tibetans.

LEFT: Lama Yeshe Dorje, the famed "weather-controller" who passed away in 1993, was known for healing mental disturbances in others by using an ancient form of exorcism. ABOVE: Whirling a hand-held drum and blowing a bone trumpet, a student of Lama Yeshe Dorje wears the white robes of a lay tantric practitioner. In the Nyingma tradition, men and women living otherwise monastic lives are free to marry; many of Tibet's most accomplished female practitioners are connected with this lineage. BOTTOM: Lama Yeshe Dorje dresses in ceremonial robes for traditional Nyingma practices.

TIBETAN SACRED ARTS
Tashi Jong

A scenic two-hour drive into the valley below Dharamsala brings the traveler to a majestic, thick-walled structure. This imposing example of classical Tibetan architecture, with its steep stairway to the main temple, is the Tashi Jong Monastery. The interior is filled with exquisite artistic detail. The monastic community itself is well-known for its sacred arts.

In a downstairs wood-carving studio, several monks work long hours sculpting ink blocks of religious figures and sacred texts. In the monastery courtyard, dozens of monks practice ritual music and dances, using Tibetan long-horns, drums, and elaborate masks and costumes. And in a private studio, a master painter creates intricate *tangka* paintings of Buddhist deities. Visitors to the Tashi Jong Monastery and its charming Tibetan village may want to make a first visit there to commission a painting and inquire about upcoming dates for sacred dancing — and then schedule a return trip to purchase the *tangka* and observe a ceremony of religious arts.

TOP: Approximately 65 miles south of Dharamsala, the Tashi Jong Monastery, a striking example of Tibetan architecture, is situated in a quiet valley and is known for its efforts to preserve the sacred arts of Tibet. BOTTOM: As two Black Hat dancers wait to enter the sacred performance, monks wearing masks of the Chinese philosopher Ha Shan and his disciples watch an early segment of the traditional 17-day Mahakala festival held at Tashi Jong Monastery. RIGHT: Transfixed by the accented rhythms and swirling costumes of the Black Hat Dance, a woman peers into a small temple at Tashi Jong Monastery. Most of the all-day purificatory ritual is executed under a large canopy in front of the main temple.

Against an orange background, a decorative painting in traditional style adorns an outer wall of the Norbulingka.

Mani stones covered with prayers adorn an outdoor shrine at the Norbulingka.

Ornate pillars and colorful walls are typical of Tibetan architectural facades but are rarely affordable in exile communities. Leading architects and artists were commissioned to build and decorate the Norbulingka Institute in the early 1990's.

CULTURAL HERITAGE
The Norbulingka

A 500-year-old Bodhi tree faces a new facility located in an idyllic haven beneath the Dhauladur range of the Himalayas. With quaint tea gardens beside meandering streams, the Norbulingka Institute was established near Dharamsala in the early 1990's to encourage the continuity of Tibet's rich and unique cultural heritage. The institute is named after the Dalai Lama's summer palace in Tibet; founded by the 7th Dalai Lama in the 18th century, it contained a school of arts and sciences. The new Norbulingka consists of two wings specializing in these fields.

The Norbulingka's Center for Arts employs master painters and sculptors trained in Tibet prior to 1959. In the early days of exile, these artists worked without sufficiently carrying out the teaching tradition, and not enough apprentices were trained to continue the chain of high artistry. Now, with proper facilities and materials, artists can pursue these specialized art forms. *Tangka* painting, clay sculpture, woodworking, and fabric work are approached as religious art forms requiring specific conditions for proper execution, just as they were in Tibet. Traditional works are sold at the center without commercial exploitation.

The Norbulingka's Center for Higher Tibetan Learning operates as a college of literature and philosophy. A major goal of this wing is to make the classic traditions accessible to the modern world. The program involves a six-year course of studies that gives Tibetan students a solid foundation for their own scholastic and literary pursuits. Classes in Buddhist philosophy, Tibetan and other Buddhist histories, poetry, and Tibetan grammar and composition emphasize historical context. The institute also offers classes for non-Tibetans and a four-year course in comparative Tibetan and Chinese Buddhist terminology. By supporting and encouraging original written work and scholarly teaching in the academic world, the center assures continuity in the evolution of Tibetan Buddhist thought.

FAR LEFT: The Norbulingka Institute, modeled after the summer residence and cultural center established in Lhasa, Tibet, in 1754 by the 7th Dalai Lama, rests on a 5-acre site near Dharamsala.

SPINNING PRAYERS AND WEAVING TAXIS
McLeod Ganj

On this bright blue September morning, a multi-layered shaft of silvery sunlight finds its way through a gap in the Himalayas, enlightening the buildings on the mountainside above Dharamsala. You squint for a moment at the simple cheeriness of it. Next stop: McLeod Ganj.

Careening around narrow bends and weaving irregularly past oncoming vehicles and meandering pedestrians, you wonder if perhaps your hired driver is trying to recreate a Tibetan carpet pattern across the wooded countryside. You step out of the taxi/mini-van in front of a roomy general store at the top of McLeod Ganj. You are standing in the heart of the refugee community, gazing with wonder on the busy center of a small town.

Drawn toward the *stupa*, a monument containing Buddhist relics, you watch two women with thickly braided hair reach out to spin metal drums suspended from the outside walls of a rectangular structure. These prayer wheels are inscribed with Tibetan characters and are believed to send positive energy throughout the world. The women pause to smile warmly at each other, the outer corners of their eyes crinkling with joy.

Uncertain whether you want to find a room for the night or a cafe for some breakfast, you arrange your bags over your shoulders and wander down the earthen road leading directly past the colorful prayer wheels. Gazing at the simple shops lining the street, you notice a smart black jacket bordered with thin stripes woven in many colors. It hangs from a piece of wood attached to a string, catching the breeze outside the open-air front entrance to a numbered shop. You note it to be amazingly inexpensive and decide to return to this shop later.

From some unknown alleyway, a hefty black cow saunters toward you. Looking furtively about, you decide to do as everyone else and pretend the beast does not exist. Swerving as inconspicuously as possible, you find yourself on the opposite side of the path. Two Tibetan children carrying books and wearing blue shirts and grey pants giggle merrily at your gracelessness. You shrug your shoulders and grin at them.

Fruit stands, cafes and small shops line the streets of McLeod Ganj. The settlement town makes its living primarily through the shops, guest houses, hotels and restaurants that cater to visitors.

As you step with embarrassment into the nearest shop, you are confronted with bins of variously colored dried beans, grains and rice. The Indian shopkeeper nods at you. Rows of toilet paper, dusty shampoo bottles and candles sit above his head. Suddenly you notice a few unwrapped round loaves of wheaty-looking bread resting on the corner of a front flour bin. You look inquiringly at the man and he nods again, asking five rupees for each loaf. Tired from your journey, you decide not to barter and pay gratefully for the top loaf. It is still warm.

On the street again, nibbling at sweet chunks of brown bread, you pass several shops filled with both trinkets and treasures. Open-air windows and doorways display large selections of lapis, turquoise, coral, and bone jewelry, or assorted Buddhist prayer implements crafted in metal. Fur-lined Tibetan hats embroidered in silk, Indian shawls of colored wool, Western-style jeans, key rings, sunglasses — all can be found in McLeod Ganj. In time you learn it is not altogether unusual to find Tibetan heirlooms for sale. Perhaps a dramatic, long-looped turquoise earring recently has been sold to a shopkeeper for income by an impoverished refugee family. It sits amid a hodgepodge of miscellaneous goods in a cluttered display case, waiting for a respectful tourist to take it home and treasure its historic and human value.

Nearing a left turn in the town's single road, you pause for a moment to consider whether to explore this new direction or continue forward. Indecisive, you stop to admire thick carpets stacked in a store on the corner. Small statues of Buddha, assorted divinities and great sages rest on shelves behind the main counter. Containers of semiprecious stones line the front cabinet. A customer selects gems and presses them into small, circular indentations on a two-foot statue of the goddess Tara. A young woman shopkeeper assures her customer that each stone will be expertly secured to its requested place on the newly purchased sacred image.

As you step outside, a group of men and women in ancient dress strolls down the rough road. With prayer beads dangling from their wrists, they turn each wooden bead with a distinctive concentration, gazing at the dust ahead while moving gently forward. You wonder if these unusually dressed Tibetan Buddhists have only recently arrived in Dharamsala from Tibet or Nepal. They seem road weary yet their weathered faces are bright with the incredibly genuine smiles you now associate with Tibetan culture. Weary yourself, you decide to find some lodging and lighten your load before adventuring further. Returning the pilgrims' smiles, you turn back toward McLeod Ganj, where you can plan your explorations into the unique culture of exiled Tibet.

Dancing in the streets, Tibetans celebrate the New Year. Week-long festivities contain both traditional folk and religious activities.

TOP LEFT: In anticipation of seeing the Dalai Lama as he passes, a woman waits in the Central Cathedral courtyard beside Namgyal Monastery. UPPER CENTER LEFT: Green stairways create a colorful playground for a young girl who lives with her family in the Tibetan Administration's residential compound below McLeod Ganj. LOWER CENTER LEFT: A married carpet trimmer poses with his teenage daughter and her friend in the small room rented by the family. Together, both parents earn the equivalent of about $5.00 per week. BOTTOM LEFT: Selling everything from fresh eggs to richly embroidered jackets, a businesswoman runs one of the only shops outside the entrance gate to the Tibetan Administration offices. LEFT: Seen from above, the town of McLeod Ganj looks like a modern city, yet awakens each morning with the chanting of Tibetans preparing for a day of business. ABOVE: An Indian delivery truck waits for Tibetan monks to complete a New Year ceremony, while Westerners observe the activities taking place on a narrow mountain street of McLeod Ganj. BELOW: Two Tibetan women haul dirt to patch potholes in the road leading to the Dalai Lama's residence. Communal spirit remains a way of life for Tibetans living in exile.

TOP: Squinting to keep out the soap, a boy is bathed on a stoop by his mother. Most families must share community water faucets. ABOVE: Literally the center of life in the business district of McLeod Ganj, the Namgyalma Stupa, encircled by prayer wheels, is a religious memorial to those who have lost their lives during the Chinese occupation of Tibet. Most residents take the time daily to turn each wheel while circling the shrine. RIGHT: A sudden October hail storm transforms McLeod Ganj into a storybook scene.

Maps and Methods: Travel Hints

Visas

Apply for your travel permit early, but remember that tourist visas are often valid from the date of issue rather than date of arrival. Visas can be renewed in India, but the process can be irritating. Your passport and

traveler's checks (which can be most easily cashed at banks) are safest when carried together in a specially made cloth pouch worn under your shirt. The pouch has a lightweight cord that goes around your neck, and is

absolutely the most theft-proof method for carrying these items. It may feel strange to travel this way at first, but you'll soon get used to it. And it's far better than being nervous all the time or stranded in South Asia without funds or travel documents.

Money

The currency exchange rate in India is continually fluxuating, but the rate as of July 1995 is approximately 30 rupees to a dollar. For immediate expenses, it is recommended that you change some money at the airport at the time of your arrival in India.

Be sure to keep your receipts each time you change money.

Making Plans

The Tibetan government-in-exile co-owns and operates a travel bureau with offices in New Delhi and Dharamsala. Potala Tours and Travels, established for the purpose of assisting foreign travelers going to Dharamsala and other Tibetan areas of India and Nepal, can arrange all or part of your journey,

including assistance with accomodations and other personalized services. From the U.S. they may be reached in New Delhi at tel. 011- 91 - 11 - 777-5242, or fax 011-91-11-371-3309.

From Delhi to Dharamsala

To get to Dharamsala, most people go first to Delhi. It is best to just enjoy India's capital city for a while, before embarking on the rather difficult trip to Dharamsala. Keep your passport handy; you never know when you'll be asked to show it. From Delhi you can reach Dharamsala by car, bus, plane or train. The car trip (with a hired driver) takes approximately 11 hours and costs about $135, which can be divided by the number of passengers willing to share the expense.* A direct bus route from Connaught Place or Tibetan New Camp, North Delhi, takes about 14 hours to

*Schedules, fares and prices are correct as of July 1995, but may quickly change.

reach Dharamsala and costs $11. Air flights leave Delhi for the Jammu airport daily; the fare is $74 one way, and the remaining trip from Jammu to Dharamsala takes 51/2 hours by car and costs an additional $70.

If you choose to travel from Delhi to Dharamsala by train, you can either take advantage of the services offered by a travel agency, or go directly to the New

Delhi train station. On the second floor is an office which deals with reservations for foreign travelers. Your reservation and ticket should be for an AC (air conditioned) first or second class sleeper to Pathankot (the closest train station to Dharamsala). Make sure you are clear which station your train leaves from, as there is also an Old Delhi station.

Three trains go daily to Pathankot; recommended is the Jammu Tawi Mail, which leaves Old Delhi Railway Station at about 9:00 P.M. and arrives in Pathankot at about 6:45 A.M. Give yourself plenty of time at the station, and be sure to bring bottled water and some food for the all-night journey.

Delhi train stations are intense with activity and can be rather confusing. Red-shirted porters will carry your luggage and find your train and seat for about 75 cents. Alternatively, when you succeed in locating the platform that your train leaves from, you'll find a notice board listing

the names of passengers and their assigned car and compartment numbers. Don't worry too much if you can't find the right car. Passengers tend to be rather pushy, so just get on the train right along with everyone else. You can always sort out the seating arrangements later.

From Pathankot, you can either hire a car and driver (3 hours), or take a rickshaw to the bus station and

then take a bus to Dharamsala (41/2 hours). Buses are typically crowded and uncomfortable but in some circles are considered essential to a true experience of India.

Places to Stay

Dharamsala has numerous hotels and guest houses, though it is good to keep in mind that at certain times of the year (notably in mid

October or late February and early March) rooms can become scarce. The moderately priced Hotel Tibet and the somewhat more expensive Hotel Bhagsu both have comparably efficient service and attached restaurants. For a quieter atmosphere try the Kongpo Guest House or the Ashoka Guest House. Chonor House has some of the nicest rooms for those who can afford its slightly higher prices.

Many of the Tibetan monasteries in the area have guest houses with simple accommodations and

low fees. Namgyal Monastery, Tse Chok Ling, Nechung Monastery, and the Nyingma Temple all have rooms for individuals who will respect a monastic setting, away from the noise of McLeod Ganj.

Additional places to stay include: the Green Guest House, the Kokonor Hotel, the Kalsang Guest House, the Kailash Hotel, the Om Hotel, the

Namgyal Guest House (different from the Namgyal Monastery Guest House), the Drepung Loseling Guest House, the Paljor Gakyil Guest House, Seven Hills Lodge, Lhasa Guest House, Himalaya Hotel, Hotel Snow Palace, International Guest House, the Hotel Natraj, and the Suriya Hotel. Hotels and guest houses are continually being built. You may find some new ones.

Places to Eat
Most restaurants offer a variety of choices in Indian, Tibetan, Chinese, and Western cuisine. Selections are generally quite simple but plentiful. Among the best places in McLeod Ganj are: the Shangrila Cafe, the Shambala Cafe, the Gakyi, the Hotel Tibet Restaurant, Dolkar Restaurant, Sangye Passang Restaurant, the Tashi Hotel Restaurant, Kailash

Hotel Restaurant, Rising Horizon Cafe, Friends Corner, and others, including a bakery known as the Chocolate Log. Below town, near the Library of Tibetan Works and Archives, there is Nechung Monastery's restaurant, where government-in-exile volunteers and others associated with the Tibetan Administration often gather. There are also several small eateries located in the homes of enterprising Tibetans.

More About Food
Always make sure the food you order is thoroughly cooked, and never drink tap water. Fresh foods should be peeled or washed meticulously with sanitized water (by boiling, or purified with iodine drops or packaged pills). It is not that the bacteria in local food is particularly bad, but rather that you do not have a built-up immunity to those types of bacteria.

If you plan to stay in India for several months or longer, you can gradually build an immunity by introducing local foods into your system.

Most of India is vegetarian, and keeping a vegetarian diet is probably a good idea while there. When in doubt about food quality or adequate protein intake, nibble generously from your pre-packaged supply of trail mix or crackers and peanut butter.

What to Bring

Everyone has their own preferred list of necessities, but traveling light is a good idea. Since pharmaceuticals are not always available throughout most of India, prepare a first aid kit stocked with such items as water purification pills, antibacterial ointment or cream, antidiarrheal medication, anti-malaria pills, aspirin or aspirin-free pain

relievers, cold and cough medicine, eye drops, adhesive tape and bandages, waterproof insect repellent, waterproof sunscreen and sunburn lotions, moistened towelettes, moisture lotion, and lip balm.

As for medications, bring a full supply of your regular prescription medicines, to last

somewhat longer than the period of time you intend to be abroad. Carry them in the original containers to identify them as legally obtained drugs and pack them in your carry-on bag.

Be sure to bring a flashlight and batteries for your evening walks or the frequent (but generally brief) power outages in India. And find yourself a leak-proof canteen or plastic hiker's bottle, to take purified water with you wherever you go.

High fashion is definitely not a priority in Dharamsala, so keep your focus on practical, all-weather clothing. Good walking shoes are a must. While India's summers are very hot, many people travel to the Himalayas with a sleeping bag, especially during the winter months or Dharamsala's

monsoon season (mid to late summer); it can be tossed over the bedding provided by most hotels and guest houses. A hood or hooded sweatshirt comes in handy, as it can either protect your neck from intense daytime sun, or help maintain body heat during chilly Himalayan evenings.

Don't bother carrying a bulky sweater, as wool sweaters are sold cheaply in Dharamsala. Fewer clothes are basically better than too many, as you can always pick up needed items along the way. Besides, it would be a good idea to save space in your luggage for those special purchases you'll be bringing back home with you.

For Further Reading

India: A Travel Survival Kit
Findlay, Crowther, Thomas and Wheeler. Lonely Planet, 1993.

Freedom in Exile: The Autobiography of the Dalai Lama
HarperCollins, 1990.

In Exile from the Land of Snows: The Dalai Lama and Tibet since the Chinese Conquest
John F. Avedon. Alfred Knopf, 1984.

My Tibet
Galen Rowell. University of California Press, 1990.

Special thanks to Sidney Piburn, Bill Warren, and Susan and Peter Campbell for their travel suggestions.

Overview of Dharamsala area (below) and McLeod Ganj (right)

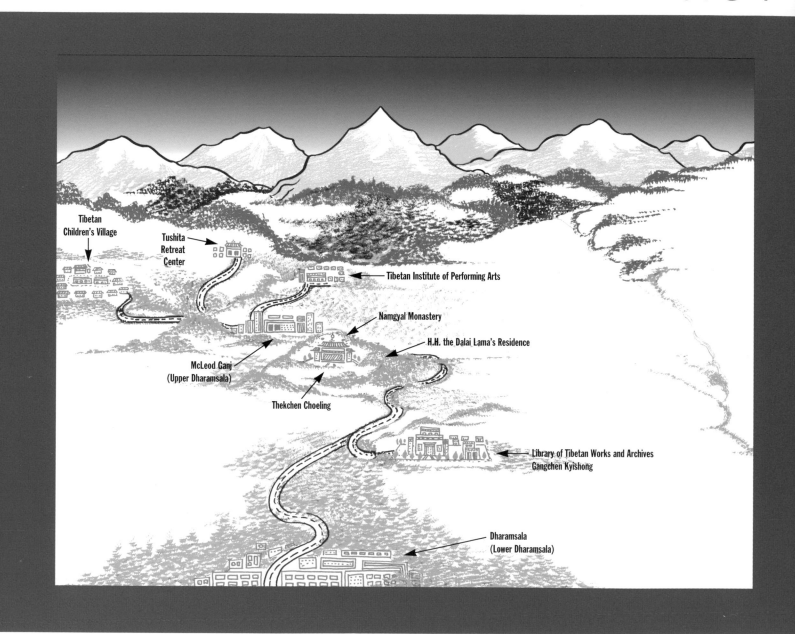

Maps by Palden Choedak Oshoe (above) and Sidney Piburn (right); design by Terrance John and Craig Korn.

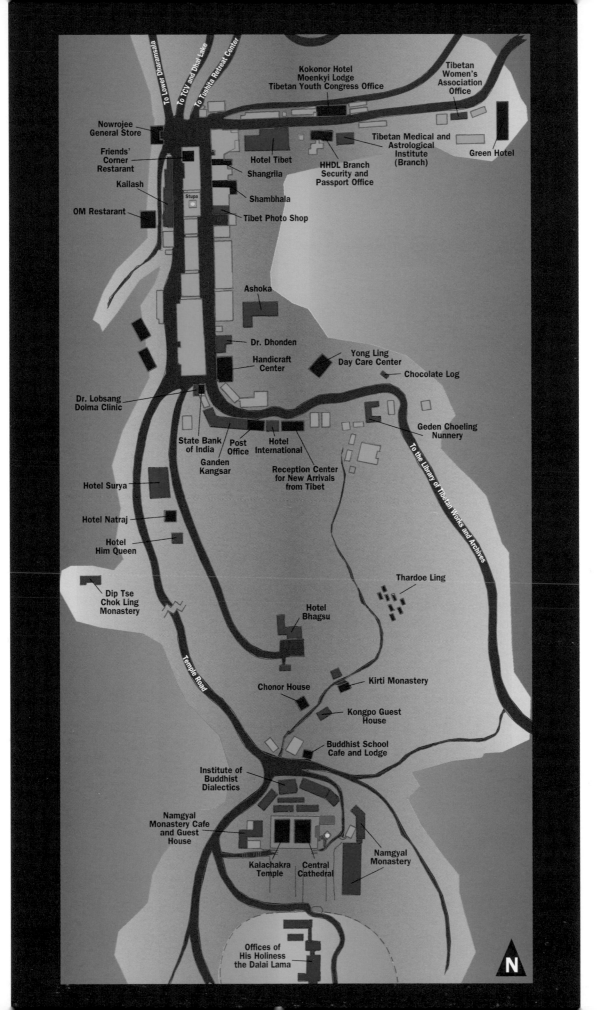

To Lower Dharamsala

To TCV and Dhal Lake

To Tushita Retreat Center

Kokonor Hotel
Moenkyi Lodge
Tibetan Youth Congress Office

Tibetan
Women's
Association
Office

Nowrojee
General Store

Hotel Tibet

Tibetan Medical and
Astrological
Institute
(Branch)

Friends'
Corner
Restarant

Shangrila

HHDL Branch
Security and
Passport Office

Green Hotel

Kailash

Shambhala

OM Restarant

Stupa

Tibet Photo Shop

Ashoka

Dr. Dhonden

Yong Ling
Day Care Center

Handicraft
Center

Chocolate Log

Dr. Lobsang
Dolma Clinic

Geden Choeling
Nunnery

State Bank
of India

Post
Office

Hotel
International

To the Library of Tibetan Works and Archives

Ganden
Kangsar

Reception Center
for New Arrivals
from Tibet

Hotel Surya

Hotel Natraj

Hotel
Him Queen

Thardoe Ling

Dip Tse
Chok Ling
Monastery

Hotel
Bhagsu

Temple Road

Kirti Monastery

Chonor House

Kongpo Guest
House

Buddhist School
Cafe and Lodge

Institute of
Buddhist
Dialectics

Namgyal
Monastery Cafe
and Guest
House

Namgyal
Monastery

Kalachakra
Temple

Central
Cathedral

Offices of
His Holiness
the Dalai Lama

N

A striking figure standing on the roof of the Zilnon Kagye Ling temple, Lama Thupten Gyatso seems to symbolize the relocation of Tibetan culture. His ceremonial hat, which the *tulku* made for his spiritual practices, is the only possession he brought on the difficult journey from Tibet to India.

ABOVE: With a technique which allows his cymbals to reverberate between each other, the Namgyal Monastery chant master sings in deep-throated tonal ranges during a late afternoon prayer ceremony at the monastery. RIGHT: A painted slogan on a closed storefront announces the determination of the exiled people of Tibet to regain their homeland. Most refugees anticipate one day moving the seat of the Tibetan government back to Lhasa, Tibet. In the meantime, Dharamsala, India, is considered the Tibetan Administration's temporary capital.

Peering through a backstage changing-tent prior to an outdoor opera performance at the Tibetan Children's Village, youngsters admire the lavish costumes worn by performers from the Tibetan Institute of Performing Arts.

134

TOP: Sunlight enlivens the mountain ranges hovering protectively over Dharamsala. While living in India, refugees from Tibet take comfort in the Himalayas, a direct connection to the rugged land from which they come. ABOVE: With the sunset as a backdrop and the monastery rooftop as their stage, Namgyal monks practice in small groups for the next morning's examination on movements from the sacred Kalachakra dance.